HOUSES & GARDENS
NEEDLECRAFT SOURCE BOOK

HOUSES & GARDENS
NEEDLECRAFT SOURCE BOOK

LINDY TRISTRAM

ANAYA PUBLISHERS LTD
LONDON

First published in Great Britain in 1994
by Anaya Publishers Ltd Strode House
44–50 Osnaburgh Street
London NW1 3ND

Editor: Patsy North
Designer: Sheila Volpe
Special photography: Patrick McLeavey
Artwork: Tony Bellue, Michael Volpe, Kate Simunek

British Library Cataloguing in Publication Data
Tristram, Lindy
Houses and Gardens Needlecraft Source Book

250 Designs for Cross Stitch, Needlepoint and Embroidery
I. Title
746.44

ISBN 1-85470-153-3

Typeset by Servis Filmsetting Ltd, Manchester
Colour reproduction by J. Film Process, Singapore
Printed and bound in China

CONTENTS

INTRODUCTION

Houses and gardens in all their diversity have been a wonderful source of inspiration for embroidery throughout the ages. A country cottage with flowers growing beside the path, a smartly painted home in a town street or a grand manor house with formal gardens – all these images can be turned into beautiful stitched pictures which will bring back fond memories of places visited and houses lived in. You don't need to go far to find ideas. Just look around your own home and the homes of your friends to find a wealth of material.

I find other people's homes fascinating and, as a designer, always carry a small notebook around with me to record the things that I like, such as interesting architectural details or a tranquil corner of the garden. Unusual windows and doors, stained glass panels, pretty tiles and fireplaces might provide inspiration indoors. An interior view doesn't need to be complicated. A simple kitchen window with pots of herbs on the sill can be charming. Walk out into the garden and you might see a beautiful hanging basket with trailing plants, a pot full of scarlet geraniums or a smartly clipped bay tree in a tub. In the vegetable garden the produce is arranged in orderly rows. Runner beans, with their bright red flowers, shoot up their poles and plump strawberries ripen in the sun.

A delightful way to remember your own home or a house with happy memories is to take a photograph and work the picture into a stitched panel. I made an embroidery of a house I lived in some years ago. As two of my children were born there, it was very special to me.

In this book my aim is to provide you with a wide variety of source material to fire your imagination, but it is also to encourage you to look around your own surroundings for ideas. For beginners I have given lots of simple outlines in each chapter to trace off and work in the stitches and colours of your choice. For experienced embroiderers there are more complicated images to which you can add your own finishing touches. You could stitch little coloured curtains behind the windows on the house outlines, or add your favourite flowers to the designs in the garden chapters, combining several images into a composition of your own.

Be brave and experiment with the thickness and texture of the thread you use. Colours are important too. For realism, try to match the colours of the thread you are using closely to whatever you are stitching. Getting the right shade of terracotta to match a flowerpot makes all the difference. However, it is equally valid to work an experimental piece with your own palette of colours.

I have also included in this book many beautiful examples of embroidered items using different techniques, threads and materials to illustrate how professional embroidery designers approach the subject of houses and gardens. Remember that it is a very personal theme and your own particular style of stitching will give your work all the more character.

OPPOSITE *This idyllic scene, with vivid herbaceous borders leading the eye towards a beautiful country home, is worked in a variety of free-style embroidery stitches.*

Chapter 1

THE HOMESTEAD

Everyone has a dream of the ideal home and for many people this is a peaceful house in the country, set in beautiful surroundings. The slower pace of rural life gives country-dwellers the time to make their homes especially pretty, with well-tended gardens full of flowers.

PREVIOUS PAGE A half-timbered house in a peaceful rural setting is depicted in appliqué with hand and machine embroidery. Layers of net suggest the shimmering surface of the water.

You don't have to be a great artist or be too detailed with your drawing to suggest the outline of a rural house. A box shape with a roof, door and windows is enough to make a traditional cross stitch pattern. The great thing about rural houses is that they are often very simple; the windows have small panes of glass, sometimes with criss-cross leading, and the doors are plain with a little wooden porch. Thatched roofs look big compared to the main shape of the house and have a soft rounded outline. Tiled or slate roofs make interesting geometric repeat patterns.

Rural houses all around the world have the same timeless appeal. Save the postcards that your friends send you from their holidays, and bring them out on a winter's evening when you need some new ideas. Compare the different styles of building, for example, American clapboard houses, Swiss chalets with long, overhanging roofs, whitewashed Mediterranean villas and little English cottages huddled together for warmth and company. A basic cottage drawing repeated in a row would look lovely embroidered in soft pastel colours around a tablecloth. What a nice way to remember a happy holiday.

Birthday cards can also be a good source of material; you can stick them in a scrapbook and soon build up a large collection. Many have pretty borders incorporated into their design which can easily be copied. Magazines, too, often yield ideas from the glossy photographs in their homes features.

This hanging of a country house is worked in appliqué and wadded quilting using a selection of plain and textured fabrics.

Needlepoint and free-style embroidery stitches are combined in this charming picture of a flower-bedecked country cottage.

Simple windows, a thatched roof and a wooden porch are all straightforward to work in free-style stitches.

One of the differences between rural homes and those in towns and cities is the amount of greenery surrounding them. If your design looks plain, trace a tree shape or a topiary hedge outline and repeat it on either side of the house. You could also stitch a row of simple flowers along the front of the house. Hollyhocks and sunflowers are good bold shapes for tall flowers. For blocks of colour in your work, think of aubrietia and alyssum in drifts of mauve and white. For a southern European scene, a gnarled, twisted grape-vine could be shown growing against a sun-baked villa and in tropical climates the plants might be passion flowers, bougainvillaea or orchids.

As an English designer, to me one of the best ways of embellishing a picture of a country cottage is to embroider romantic roses around the door. When you have completed your cottage design, work the greenery around the door in stem stitch, then work the roses in French knots or groups of bullion knots and the leaves in another free-style stitch. Try to portray the random path taken by the plant as it weaves its way around the doorway. Can you imagine the perfume of the flowers as you admire your finished piece?

Plastic canvas is the basis of this three-dimensional free-standing cottage stitched in woollen yarn. The roof can lift off to reveal a storage box.

Rural scenes make lovely needlepoint pictures. Use soft country colours for this pair of cottages.

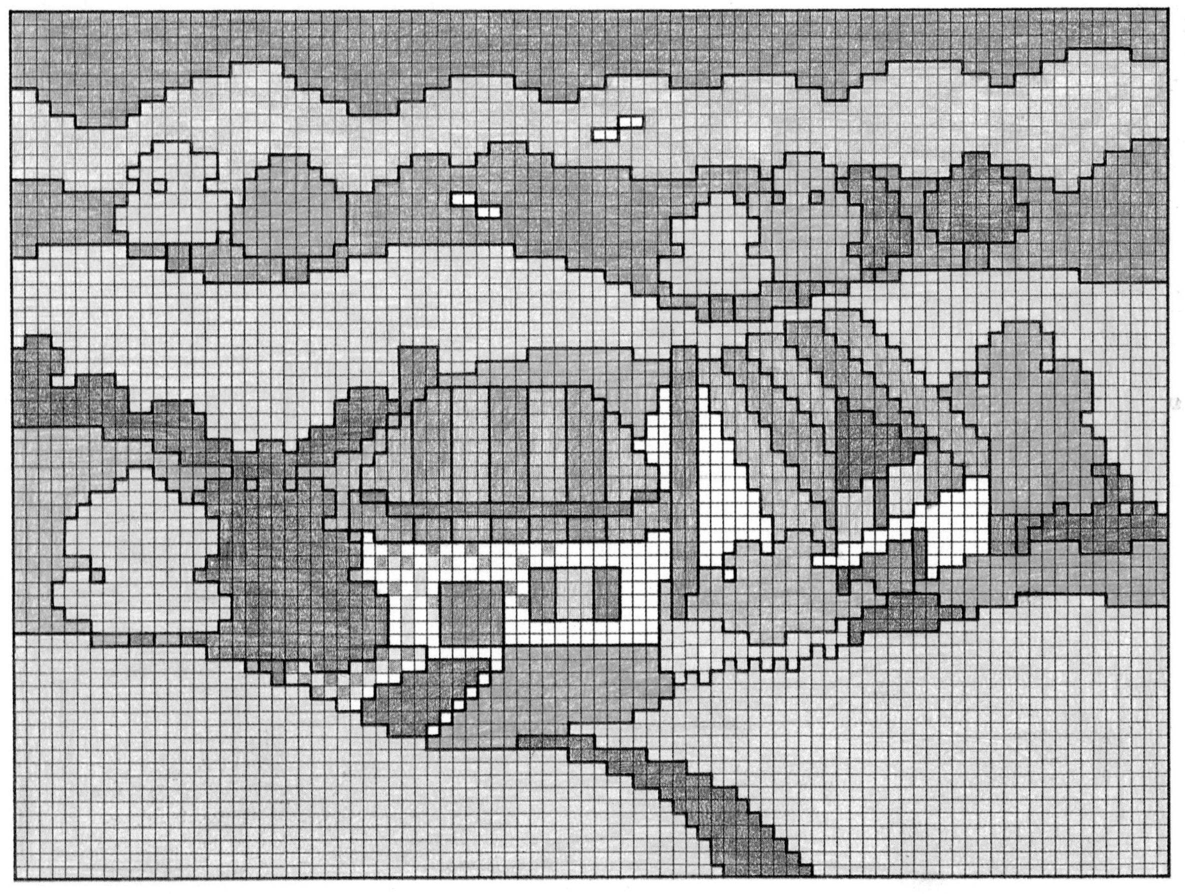

Embroidered cottages, with their romantic appeal, can be used to decorate items all around the home, especially table linen such as place mats and runners. They also make delightful pictures with an old-fashioned charm. The thatched cottage in cross stitch would look very pretty with rambling roses added after the main design has been worked. Use bullion knots and French knots to add texture.

The jolly scarecrow could add fun to simple appliqué curtains in a child's nursery, and you could continue the theme by stitching little birds all along the edge of a pillowcase and quilt cover.

Running rabbits, hopping birds and galloping horses add a humorous touch to your work and can be used singly or as lively borders. Try using these motifs in free-style embroidery on a child's jumper or dungarees. The rabbits, if enlarged, would work very well as appliqué motifs edged with blanket stitch on a baby's lightly padded quilt. The little birds could be embroidered along the scalloped edge of a baby's blanket.

Cottages are always such appealing images and can be used time and again for many items. Add details of your own, such as coloured curtains at the windows or your favourite flowers in the garden. A pretty maid drawing water from a well has a traditional feel and could be part of a rural scene.

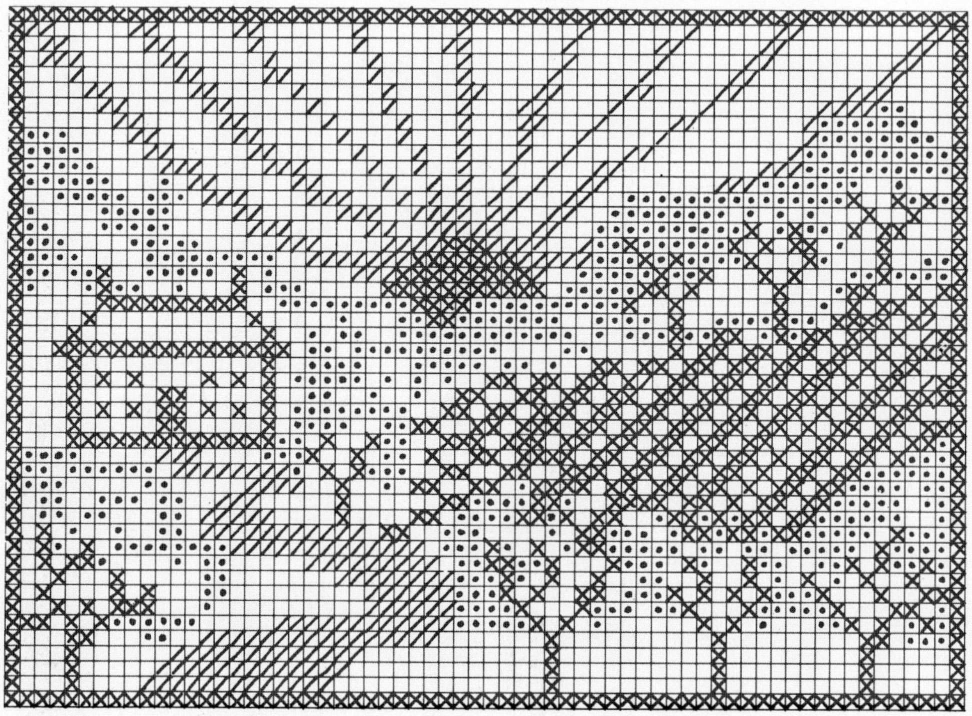

With these designs you can add interest to all kinds of ordinary household items, especially in the kitchen. The outlines of the tiny cottages would look lovely embroidered in simple back stitch on to tea towels or tablecloths. You could use plain, bright colours for the doors and windows and soft, muted shades for the walls and thatched roofs. The windmills would make a bold cross-stitch design for a nursery picture or could make a special present if they were worked singly on to a pair of oven gloves. Alternatively, use the chart to work the windmill motif in cross stitch on to the pocket of a child's gingham dress.

The Swiss village scene was copied from a postcard and would look enchanting worked in fine free-style embroidery. This scene could easily be incorporated into a much bigger picture of a mountain view.

Chapter 2

TOWNS AND CITIES

Towns and cities offer a wealth of inspiration for embroidery with their large and imposing buildings as well as their streets of houses, both grand and modest. In the older parts of a city you will find the most decorative architecture with ornate carvings, stone pillars and other embellishments, but modern buildings also make interesting subjects with the simplicity of their geometric shapes.

I love the hustle and bustle of city life. Living in London there is no limit to the beautiful buildings from which I can take my embroidery ideas. In and around the city centre I can find styles ranging from Tudor and Georgian houses to exciting new developments which use glass and metal to great effect for maximum visual impact. Tall modern buildings are often built of reflective materials which can set up fascinating patterns for embroidery.

When you next visit a city or large town, look above the modern shop fronts and façades and you will be amazed at what you see. Fine architectural details still exist: beautiful mouldings in stone, columns and even gargoyles. Try combining some of these patterns to make an original piece of work. You can vary your approach, whether traditional or modern, by using different threads, fabrics, stitches and techniques. Counted thread work is most suitable for the symmetry of modern buildings, whereas free-style embroidery might better express the flowing lines of the more ornate architecture of earlier times.

PREVIOUS PAGE A cityscape, such as this example in needlepoint, can reveal many different styles of architecture from industrial buildings to cultural centres.

ABOVE A small town house is quick and easy to work in needlepoint. A house portrait such as this would make a delightful present for a friend.

RIGHT The geometric shapes of these town houses have been emphasized with various needlepoint stitches.

In towns, houses are often arranged in elegant terraces or tree-lined boulevards. Many have decorative railings which suggest lovely border patterns, one of which I have drawn on page 27. Others have rows of arched windows, pretty balconies or elaborate gables which make regular repeat patterns that can be used as sources for abstract designs. Taken out of context, these patterns can look surprisingly different from their original forms.

This clapboard house is worked in long stitch on canvas, with the addition of French knots for the flowers.

On holiday you may have the chance to visit a historic town or city. You will find that some areas are very old and full of interest. Walk away from the centre of the city into the winding back streets and you may see doors and windows that haven't changed for hundreds of years. When I travelled around Morocco, the cities there had a great impact on me. My favourite city was Marrakesh. Parts of the city are steeped in history. The souks have not changed in centuries and the splendour of the royal palaces could inspire a thousand embroideries.

When you travel abroad, visit the tourist information centre; they will have lots of free guides and brochures that you can take away with you, as well as all the postcards you can buy. With your own photographs, these will be a design resource that you can dip into when you return home and start developing your own ideas.

If you are planning a design of a street scene in embroidery, remember that people, and vehicles too, are an integral part of city life. Adding a figure or two to an embroidered picture will give it atmosphere and scale.

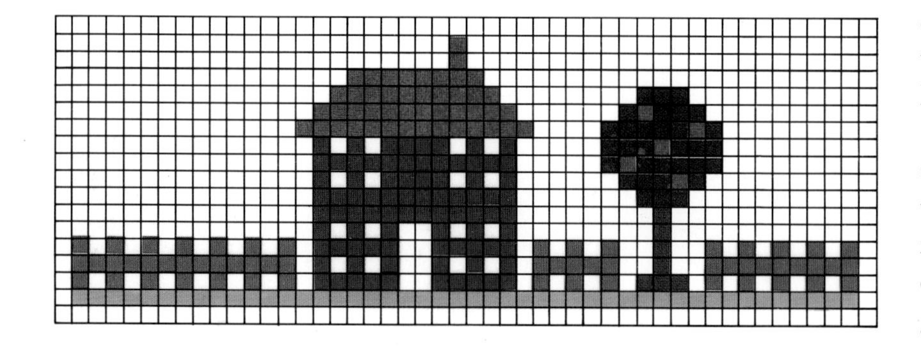

RIGHT AND OPPOSITE
Streets of houses worked in cross stitch make unusual borders for table linen or samplers. A single row of houses would look effective along the edge of a blind.

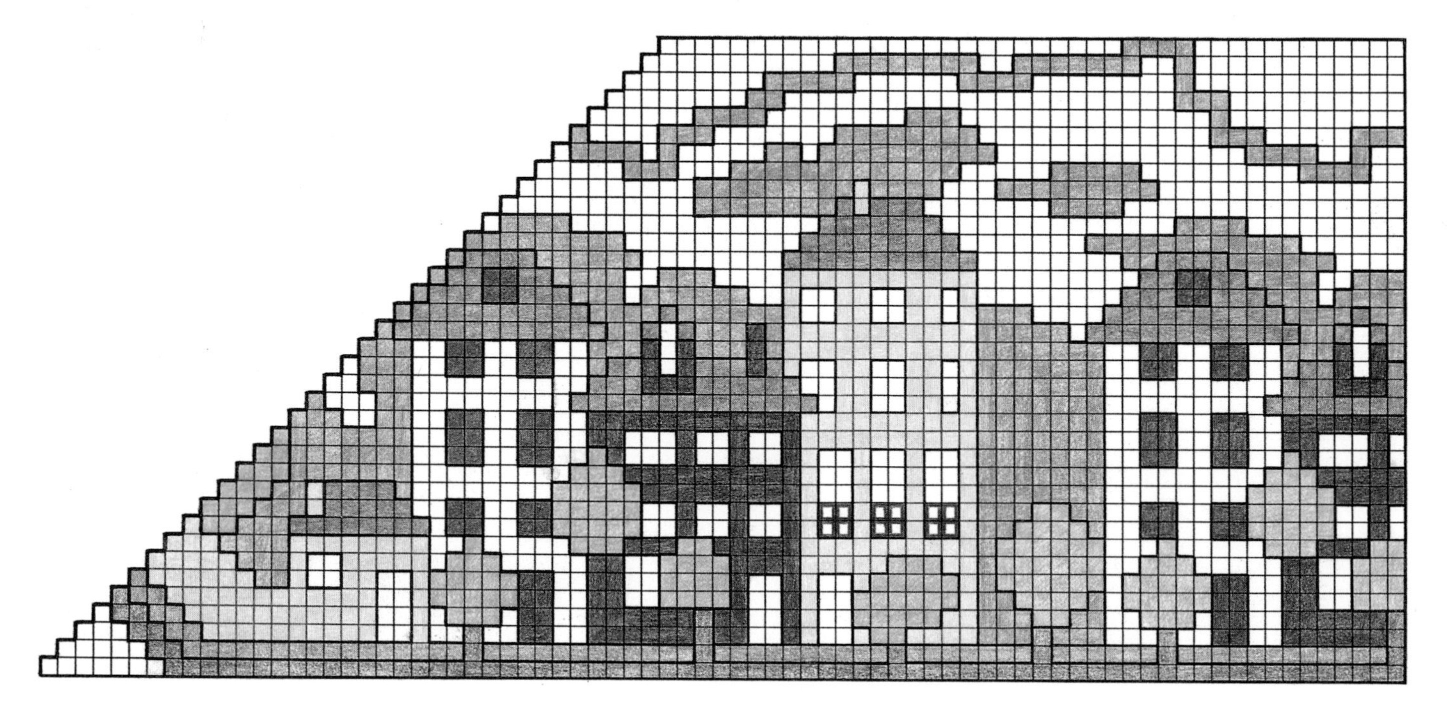

For borders and individual pictures, use the motifs inspired by towns and cities on these two pages. The two Victorian houses at the bottom of the opposite page are good images for free-style embroidery, or could quite easily be plotted on to graph paper for a cross-stitch sampler, working a border around them and placing letters and numerals in a block underneath.

The New York skyscraper and the Greek column have a hard-edged graphic quality and are interesting enough to work as embroidery designs in their own right. For an abstract design you might like to use the fanlight and window variations, outlining them or filling them in completely. The row of houses is a more complicated piece of work; try using free-style stitches including satin stitch.

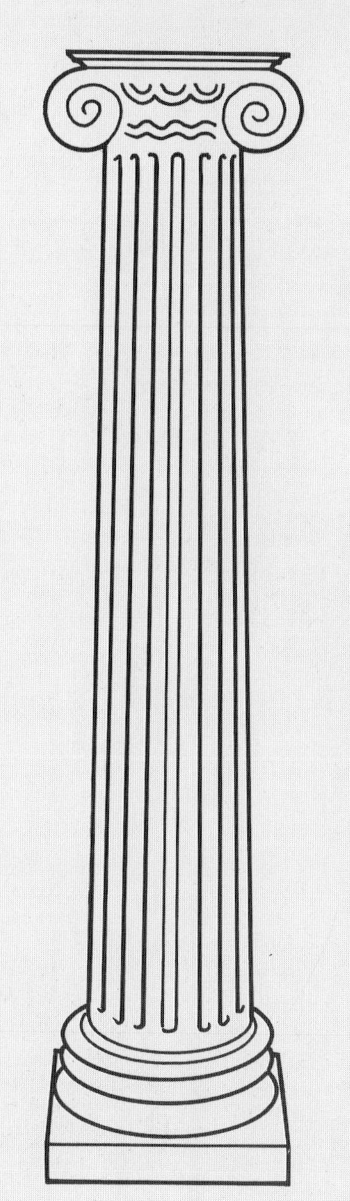

These images taken from different cities around the world lend themselves to pictures or to decorating household items, depending on the scale at which you use them. The border design of Georgian shop fronts would add an unusual touch to a tablecloth, worked in back stitch or split stitch with some couched areas. The city skyline in cross stitch could be worked in dark shades lit up with white or silver crosses for the windows. It would make an unusual wall panel for a city lover. The gabled houses stitched in cheerful primary colours or in pastels can be used in the kitchen and nursery alike, while the two walled cities would look realistic embroidered in soft, sandy shades of brown and yellow.

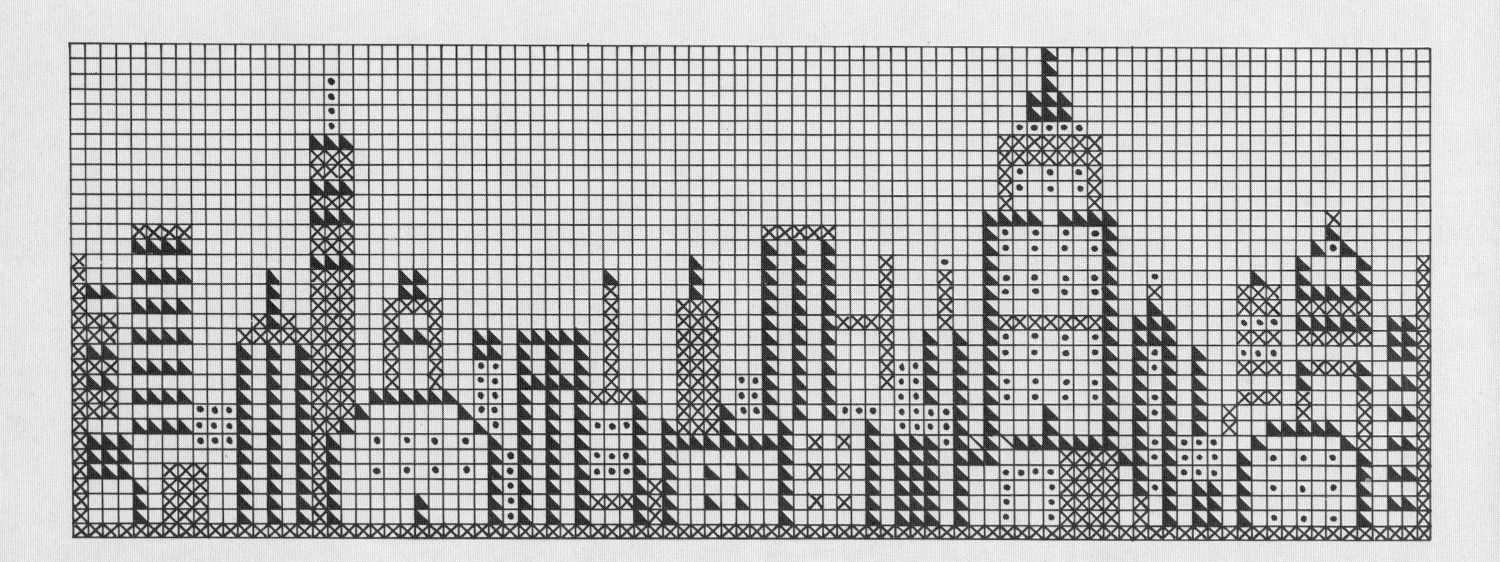

Chapter 3

DOORS AND WINDOWS

Doors and windows are two of the main architectural elements that give a house its overall style, and can be the prettiest exterior features of any home. They come in so many different sizes, shapes and colours from arched windows with stained glass to tiny dormer windows, and from elegant panelled front doors to cottage porches framed with climbing plants.

PREVIOUS PAGE The door and windows are the predominant features of this country house worked sampler-style in counted cross stitch.

The size and shape of our doors and windows depend very much on which part of the world we live in. Not only do they let people, animals and light in, but they keep things out too. In hot countries the windows tend to be smaller than in cooler climates, with heavy shutters to keep out the midday sun. In areas prone to flooding, you will find the windows are placed high up on the buildings and the doors are often at the top of a flight of steps.

Many centuries ago, if you were rich, your front door might have been a portcullis with a drawbridge. Your window would have been a slit in a stone wall to stop an arrow landing on your dining table! Not until the invention of glass did windows become large and decorative, providing more than a simple wooden shutter. Doors became smaller as there was no longer a need to bring your horse and carriage in at night, and life became more civilized.

Today we use our windows and doors decoratively as well as functionally. We paint them all the colours of the rainbow, add window boxes, pretty shutters and stained glass panels, ornate door knockers and hanging baskets.

The regular pattern of a lattice-work window is portrayed in cross stitch. It forms a monochrome background to a colourful vase of flowers.

Three different window styles are realistically interpreted in fabric collage on this interesting building.

The details of the carvings above the door and windows of this grand house are worked in free-style embroidery stitches added afterwards over the fine needlepoint background.

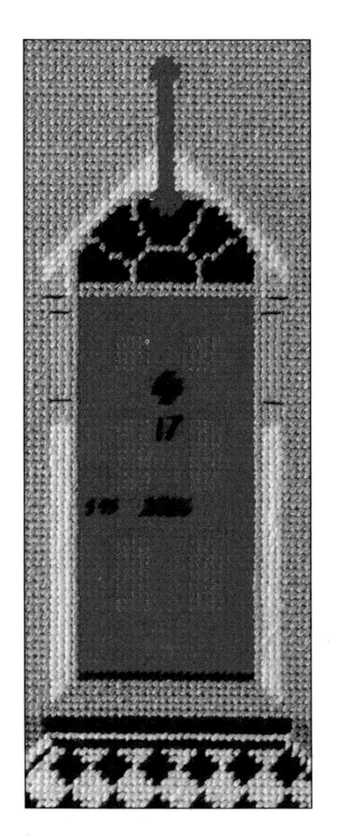

Appliqué is a useful technique for portraying doors and windows. Cut pieces of fabric to the basic shape and use simple line stitches such as running stitch or back stitch to work the detail. A straightforward house design with large windows and door would lend itself beautifully to items in a playroom or a child's bedroom. For the flowers around the door and in the window boxes you have great scope for using satin stitch with French knots, bullion knots and detached chain stitch in a chunky yarn, adding cretan, feather or fly stitches for the foliage. Emphasize different textures by using a variety of shiny and woollen threads.

A nice idea with a personal touch for friends who are moving house is to stitch them an embroidered picture of their front door. As the front door is one of the features of your house that you see daily, it's a good way of remembering your old home.

Being regular in shape, different designs of windows arranged in rows would make a good subject for a sampler in cross-stitch or needlepoint. Alternatively, you could depict them in a cheerful contemporary design using bright colours and simple shapes with machine embroidery.

Doors and windows have their own characteristic style from country to country, and from region to region. They will give you an inexhaustible supply of ideas, whether you use them alone or as part of a larger design.

ABOVE *A smartly painted town door makes an interesting image to work in needlepoint, and could form part of a sampler of different door styles.*

RIGHT *Doors make charming pictures in their own right. This example in cross stitch has an attractive porch complete with hanging basket.*

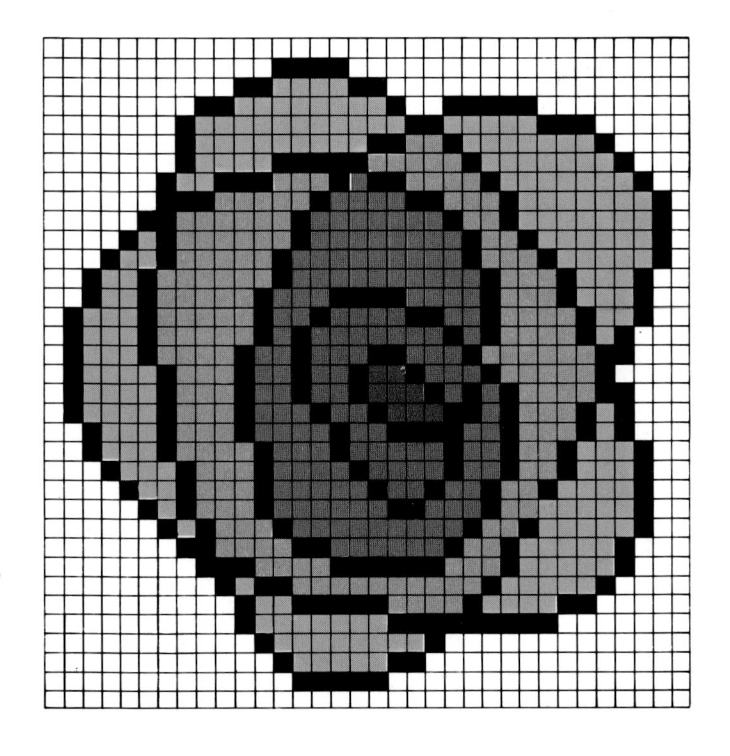

This stylized rose motif in cross stitch is based on stained glass work on a window of the Art Nouveau period.

DOORS AND WINDOWS

This selection of motifs taken from doors and windows can be used in an abstract way as patterns on articles around the home, from table linen and curtain tie-backs to cushions and pictures. On the door designs, a good way to create a three-dimensional effect is to fill in areas in satin stitch worked in different directions; this creates a variety of tones as the light is reflected from the stitches in different ways. The window designs can be represented in a realistic way by using rich colours such as reds, blues and greens to look like stained glass. Alternatively, with their simple outlines, they are perfect motifs for quilting designs.

The window design of the sunrise and bluebird is taken from a 1920s door and can be worked in a realistic way by outlining it in black and blocking it in with rich colours. The cats at the window make a humorous picture, and could be embroidered or appliquéd to make a perfect gift for a cat lover. The border design at the bottom of the opposite page would add an Eastern feel to a gathered skirt, worked in gold and silver thread and glass beads. The cross-stitch design of the roses around the front door is a very simple project for a beginner, and lends itself to further embellishment with French knots and back stitch to personalize the design. The two window motifs next to it would also make good designs for a beginner in free-style embroidery or appliqué.

8

G.A.J.

Chapter 4

ARCHITECTURE AND DECORATION

All around the world and through the ages, homes have been built in distinctive architectural styles. Columns, pediments, cornices, mouldings, carved banisters and other decorative features indoors and outdoors provide ideas for embroidery and give you the scope to explore colours and threads you may not have tried before.

PREVIOUS PAGE
Decorative features inside and outside the house set the scene for this glimpse into life in Regency times, worked as a cross stitch sampler.

Architecture and domestic ornamentation have inspired artists for hundreds of years, and decorative buildings can often be seen in the background of fine paintings. Architectural features can easily be adapted to make unusual designs in free-style embroidery, cross-stitch or needlepoint. For example, the pattern of a stone moulding, hand-stitched in a variety of threads, would make a charming panel which could be used as a tie-back for curtains. Alternatively, a tiny cross-stitch design of a gargoyle would make an unusual pin cushion.

Begin by doing a realistic drawing of the feature you wish to represent, then simplify the lines as much as possible. If you find this hard to do, use a trick of mine and turn your paper upside-down so that the drawing becomes an abstract shape which is easier to pare down to the essential lines. Try repeating the outline in a row for a border design. You can use the whole image or just a small part of it, tracing off the portion which makes the most interesting shape on its own.

How you then interpret the tracing is up to you. One option is to stitch just the outline in back stitch, stem stitch or chain stitch. This method is particularly good if you are a beginner, as you will quickly get an impressive finished piece of work. Another option is to create a three-dimensional effect by using satin stitch in colours which change in tone to represent the light and shaded areas. This shaded effect can also be achieved by changing the angle at which the stitches are worked. This creates a very unusual and subtle design.

Architectural features such as roofs, chimneys, pillars and archways can be worked realistically by using a variety of stitches to convey the textures and patterning found on them. Roofs, for example, may have different arrangements of slates or tiles, while chimneys may have been built with decorative brickwork. Needlepoint stitches are particularly effective for this.

Architectural details such as roof tiles or chimneys can be interpreted in interesting textured needlepoint stitches.

The highly decorative façade of this house in the Yemen is worked in hand and machine stitching over an appliqué and spray-painted background.

The distinctive black-and-white patterns of Tudor-style architecture are realistically interpreted here in fabric collage.

Every country has its own tradition of decorative design. The Egyptians had hieroglyphics, the Romans mosaics made from hundreds of tiny coloured pieces and the Greeks acanthus-leaved stonework. There are lots of wonderful images to trace off from books not only on architecture and design, but also on history or travel, and holiday brochures will give you more ideas. A trip to your local museum could also dig up some useful finds!

If you have an interest in architecture or decoration, you will find inspiration wherever you live, from old or new houses. Walk around your local area with a camera or sketch-pad and focus in on unusual features such as ornamental chimney pots, roof tiles, gables, porches or verandahs. Then use L-shaped pieces of card which you can move around on your picture or drawing to isolate a pleasing shape.

A simple design taken from an architectural or decorative feature could be placed inside a different shape such as a circle, a square, a diamond or an oval and then repeated all around the edge of a larger piece of work. You could use beautiful metallic thread to add sparkle to your embroidery, and textured knitting wool in muted colours to give an interesting aged effect. You could have some fun and choose the colours of your stranded cotton or tapestry wool at random. Who knows, you may find the best colour combination you have ever tried! Using some of these ideas, you can make decorative architectural images from around the world into unusual and beautiful embroideries for your home.

This Mediterranean villa has brightly coloured shutters and terracotta roof tiles typical of the region.

Egyptian hieroglyphics are great fun to embroider. You could make up your own symbols to represent the letters of a name, and stitch them on to a natural fabric such as calico to suggest papyrus. The ornate niche opposite makes a perfect frame for commemorative details of a wedding or an anniversary. The cameo design can be stitched as a simple outline or filled in with long-and-short stitch. Or try using silk appliqué for the woman's robe to create a three-dimensional effect. Use couching, chain stitch or satin stitch for the frame, perhaps in gold or silver metallic thread. The border designs on this page can be repeated on many items around the home and would also make elegant patterns on silk or satin for an evening bag or stole.

The simple, bold lines of the design on the right, taken from a conservatory, would suit a beginner using a basic outline stitch such as back stitch or split stitch, and blocked in with areas of satin stitch. If you are feeling creative, add some plants to be glimpsed through the windows. The mosaic design opposite gives enormous scope to experiment with colours, and can be enlarged and used really big with machine appliquéd squares of fabric. The sun clock is a traditional design and can be embellished with gold and silver thread. The border designs will work well in embroidery or appliqué on accessories such as scarves or bags, or on cuffs or skirt hems.

XII
I
II
III
IIII
V
VI
VII
VIII
IX
X
XI

Chapter 5

INTERIORS

The interiors of our homes are where we reveal our true personalities. The furniture, fabric and ornaments make our own home individual even if it is in a row of other similar houses. Pretty curtains, a vase of flowers on a table, cheerful pots and pans hanging up in the kitchen, or decorative china on a wooden dresser can all be translated into needlepoint, cross stitch or free-style embroidery.

PREVIOUS PAGE A view from the inside through a pretty curtained window always makes a pleasing picture. This interior is worked in needlepoint.

To find inspiration for designs based on the interiors of houses, keep your eyes open whenever you are invited into other people's homes. It always amazes me just how diverse interiors can be, with different colour schemes, furniture and decoration. They may be plain and simple or, like my own house, packed full of knick-knacks. Domestic items make charming samplers and you can introduce a personal touch by including a member of the household in the picture, or even the family pet. These figures can be as simple and as stylized as you like.

You might also like to visit historic houses for a view of a grander life-style. Here you will see rooms with furnishings that are historically correct for the period, right down to the knifes and forks in the kitchen drawer. You can also go to your local library and leaf through interior decoration books for ideas. Note down the use of colours that you like in a particular setting and photocopy pictures of interesting pieces of furniture and ornaments. I collect decorating and furnishing catalogues which can be cut up and re-arranged to plan different designs.

A modern interpretation of a tea-set shows a strong sense of design and bold colour contrasts.

RIGHT All your best-loved household items can be brought into a border around a sampler like this example in cross stitch.

OPPOSITE What could be cosier than cats basking in front of a blazing fire? Work a favourite room in free-style embroidery in a selection of stitches.

This lively bathroom scene is fun to work. It has a striped background embellished with simple embroidery stitches.

If you enjoy exploring antique shops, you will find examples of fabrics and furniture from all over the world. There might be English chintzes in soft pinks and greens, stark black-and-white patterns from Japan and elaborately embroidered fabrics in gold, silver and purple from the Middle East which will suggest new colour schemes to you. You will find that the ornaments and items of furniture are just as varied and may give you ideas for unusual embroidery designs. For instance, you could embark on a study of clocks from around the world, or stitch a piece of needlepoint showing a selection of highly decorated cups and saucers.

If you are interested in history, you could visit archeological sites, as they often have small museums displaying

Cats always make a house feel like home. This matching pair decorates a needlepoint pin cushion.

household items which have been excavated and which could be sketched and incorporated into a very unusual piece of work. You could trace off simple shapes, varying them in size and overlapping them, turning some at an angle or positioning them at random. Use threads in muted colours and fabrics such as unbleached calico in natural tones, perhaps allowing the fabric to fray slightly at the edges before mounting the finished embroidery and placing it behind glass.

Another idea for an effective design is to capture the view from the interior of a house, imagining yourself looking out through a curtained window or a half-open door. This gives a new angle on a familiar scene and adds a natural frame to the picture.

The cheeky cat sitting on the shelves would look as effective in appliqué as it would simply outlined or filled in with long-and-short stitch. Copy the colour of a friend's cat to make an extra-special gift. Teddies are always fun for children's items. Using soft pastel colours, appliqué them on to a white towel or a plain bib to make a gift for a new baby, or try embroidering them in woollen yarn in darker colours on to an older child's cardigan.

The candle can be very simply embroidered on to the pocket of a dressing gown or pyjamas for an appropriate night-time motif. For a more ambitious design, the elaborate curtains would make a picture in their own right, or could form part of a Victorian interior.

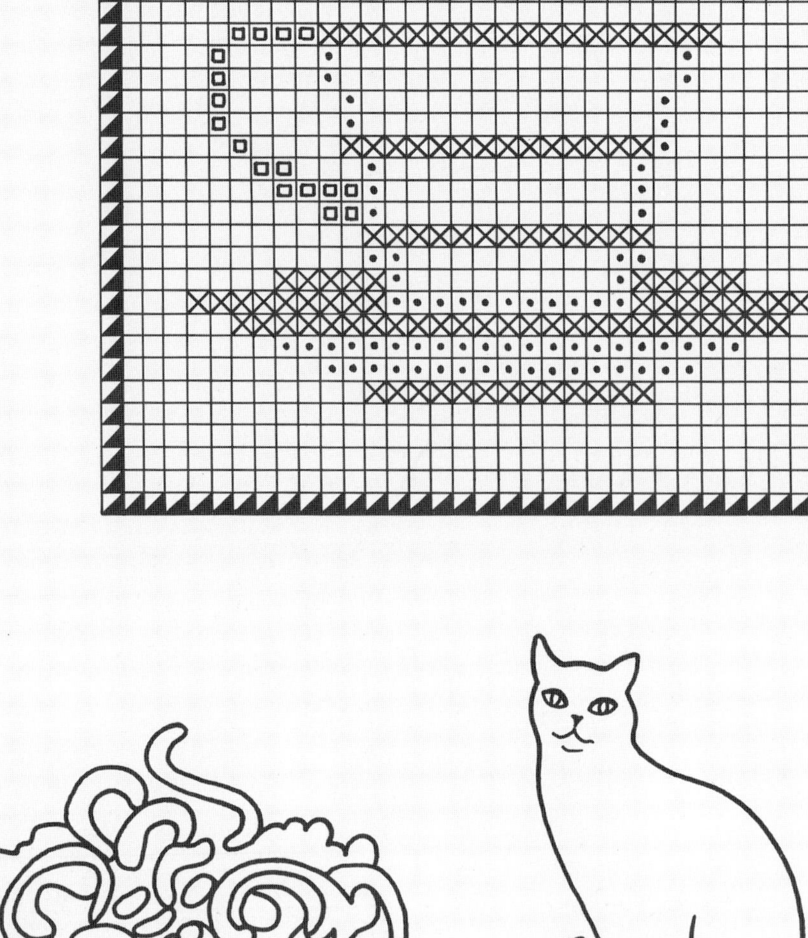

Ordinary everyday items can have a lot of style. Use these motifs all around the kitchen or dining room to add a touch of individuality to your home. The cross-stitch teacup and teapot designs would look just right on a tray cloth made of evenweave fabric, while the spoons and forks would liven up a tea towel, stitched in white on to a bright background. Enlarge the cat design to add interest to a kitchen chair cushion, working it in appliqué in cotton fabrics for ease of washing. The picture frame could be repeated several times, using a different design in the centre of each one, perhaps some family portraits! Create a personal picture in another way by outlining the image of the tea-tray and adding your own favourite flower motifs to decorate the pieces of china.

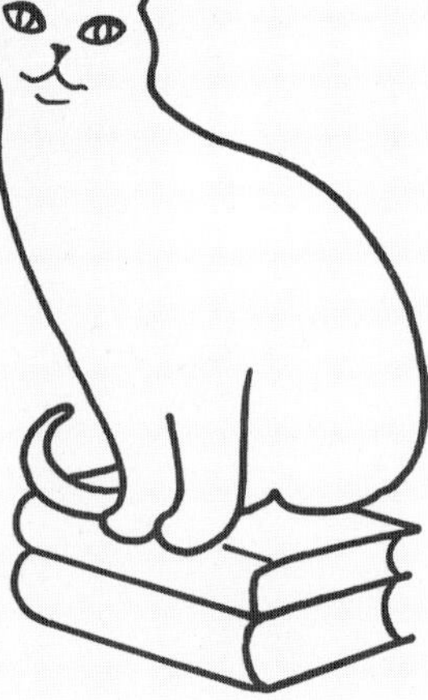

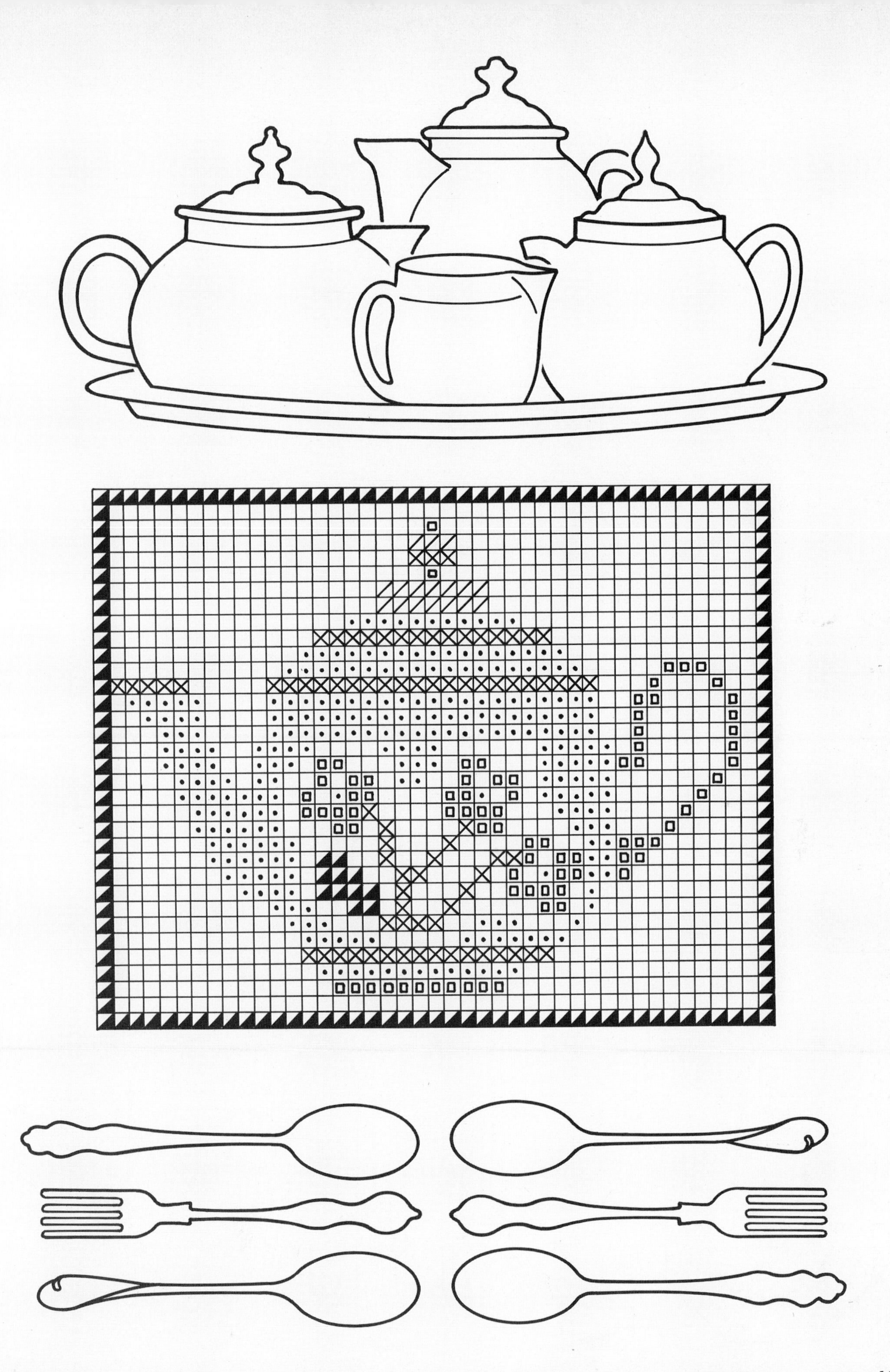

You can make an interior scene more personal by adding small touches of your own. For example, stitch a homely fire into the grate of the fireplace and add your own ornaments to the mantelpiece. The rocking horse can be used to make lovely coordinating items for the nursery, on bed linen, cot bumpers, quilts and curtains. You could combine fabric painting with the stitching for added depth of colour. The plate designs would make an unusual sampler or a bell-pull. Try adding to the patterns yourself.

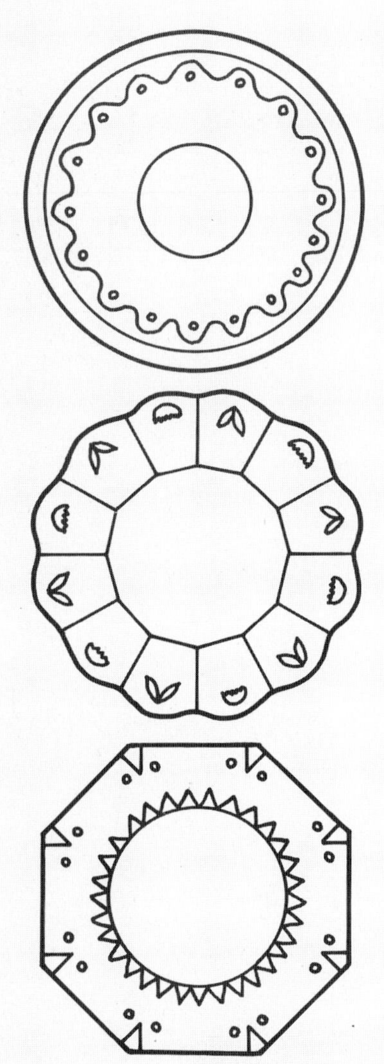

Chapter 6

TERRACES AND TUBS

Sitting out on the terrace on a warm summer afternoon is one of the pleasures of having a garden. Picture the vivid colours of geraniums and lobelia spilling out of terracotta pots or hanging baskets. You are surrounded by delicately perfumed flowers and the gentle humming of bees. Butterflies flit from plant to plant. Passion-flowers scramble up the trellis. The terrace is a lovely place to sit and work on your embroidery.

PREVIOUS PAGE Taking refreshments on the terrace is a pleasant summer pastime. The garden furniture and the roses are worked in appliqué with additional hand and machine embroidery.

FAR RIGHT Appliqué with machine embroidery are the techniques used to portray this collection of flowerpots with trailing plants.

RIGHT The charm of this needlepoint design lies in its balanced simplicity and its appealing animal and plant motifs in soft colours.

Imagine a sun-baked terrace with climbing vines and tropical flowers in tubs. If you are lucky enough to live in a hot climate, a terrace is likely to be an important part of your home where you may take your siesta in the shade of a pergola and eat your meal in the warm evening air.

Embroiderers have always taken inspiration from the natural world of flowers and plants, and a pot-grown garden or terrace is an easily accessible place for everyone. Even if you don't have a garden, some terracotta pots on your balcony, window sill or the kitchen table are just as good.

In London, where I live, my terrace is one of my favourite places, although it can only be used in the fine weather. I have pots of herbs which are close to the kitchen for ease of collection when I am preparing meals, and large tubs with fig and bay trees growing on a south-facing wall next to the house. I also grow standard roses and sweet peas round a white trellis arch which leads on to the lawn.

A design of a terrace with pots and tubs could be developed into a needlepoint picture, bringing in a variety of textures and colours. Alternatively, try taking one simple pot shape and repeating it several times, filling it with different plants each time.

Free-style embroidery stitches bring this scene of a sunny terrace to life. The hills in the background add a sense of place and give the picture perspective.

The stone urn in the foreground of this exquisite picture is embroidered with very delicate machine stitching to emphasize the contours and detail in the sculpted pattern.

Many magazines have whole features dedicated to terraces, pots and tubs which you can collect for ideas. There are so many different kinds of containers – stone urns, old lead cisterns, wooden barrels, terracotta pots both plain and decorative. They may be weathered or covered in moss, and might be arranged in formal lines or informal groups. With such a variety of textures there is scope for the use of unusual yarns, perhaps combined with fabric paints or appliqué. Your designs don't have to be elaborate; some of the simplest drawings of flowers and leaf shapes make the most interesting patterns and can be used for quilting as well as embroidery.

Other items that you might like to include in a terrace setting are outdoor furniture such as an ornate cast-iron table or some wickerwork chairs, or homely gardening tools like trowels, forks and a watering can.

If you go abroad on holiday, your hotel or villa may well have a terrace with plants and furniture different to your own at home, so don't forget to pack a sketch-book when you travel. The Mediterranean countries, such as Italy, Greece and the South of France have beautiful terraces where exotic flowers grow in profusion. Closer to home, many landscaped gardens and stately homes which are open to the public have fine examples of terraces and container gardens. Here you can sketch and take photographs as well as having a lovely day out.

A pot of geraniums is a colourful motif to decorate the corner of a small tablecloth. It is worked in a combination of satin stitch, back stitch, running stitch and French knots.

You can use these designs of container-grown plants time and time again all around the home. They make lovely motifs for your own clothes and linen as well as pretty gifts for friends. The humorous cats on the opposite page are just right to stitch on to jeans, jackets and dungarees for children. The butterflies can be delicately dotted across a tablecloth with a terracotta pot stitched in the centre, while the lemon tree or bay tree designs would look pretty embroidered on curtains.

The charted design of the tree in a planter can be stitched in needlepoint or cross stitch, adding bright red fruit. Worked on very fine canvas, it would become reduced in size and could be made into a keyring tag, for example.

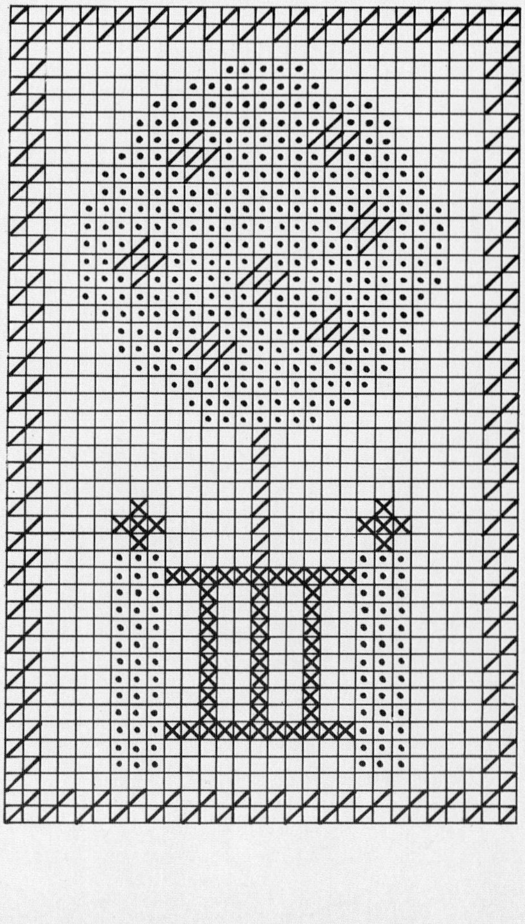

A terracotta tub bursting with fresh herbs makes a lovely design for a picture for the kitchen. Build up your work using stem stitch, back stitch, feather stitch and fly stitch for the foliage. Then add details with satin stitch, straight stitch and French knots. On the floral trellis design, make the trellis from applied ribbon, then add a splash of your favourite colour for the roses. The garden furniture and sundial make perfect accessories to include in a picture on a garden theme.

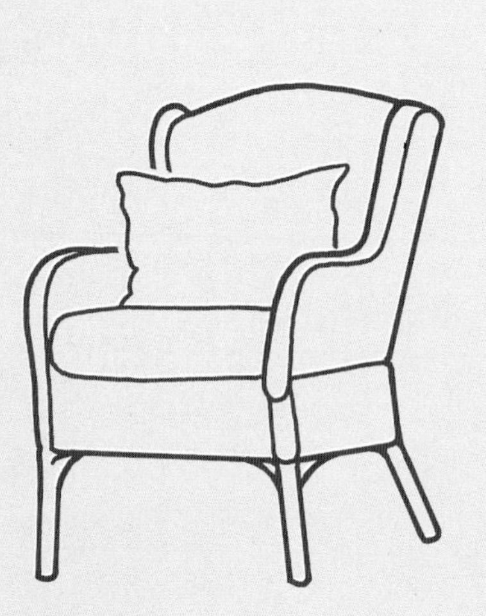

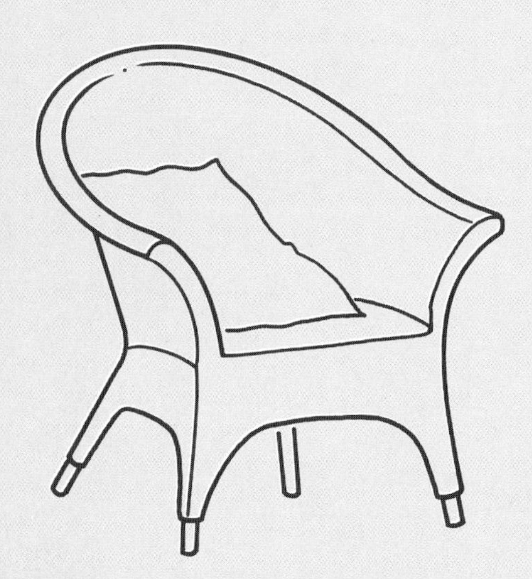

Pots and tubs of flowers are always popular and versatile motifs for all kinds of articles and give you a chance to indulge in some unusual colours and stitches. The images here would look beautiful worked in bright colours to add interest to plain linen in the kitchen and dining room. Use shades of terracotta and brown for the pots, various hues of green for the foliage and your favourite colours for the flowers.

Some of these designs are very simple and suitable for beginners. More experienced embroiderers might prefer to fill a pot with their own choice of flowers. The charted pot of flowers opposite would make a charming little picture in cross stitch or needlepoint.

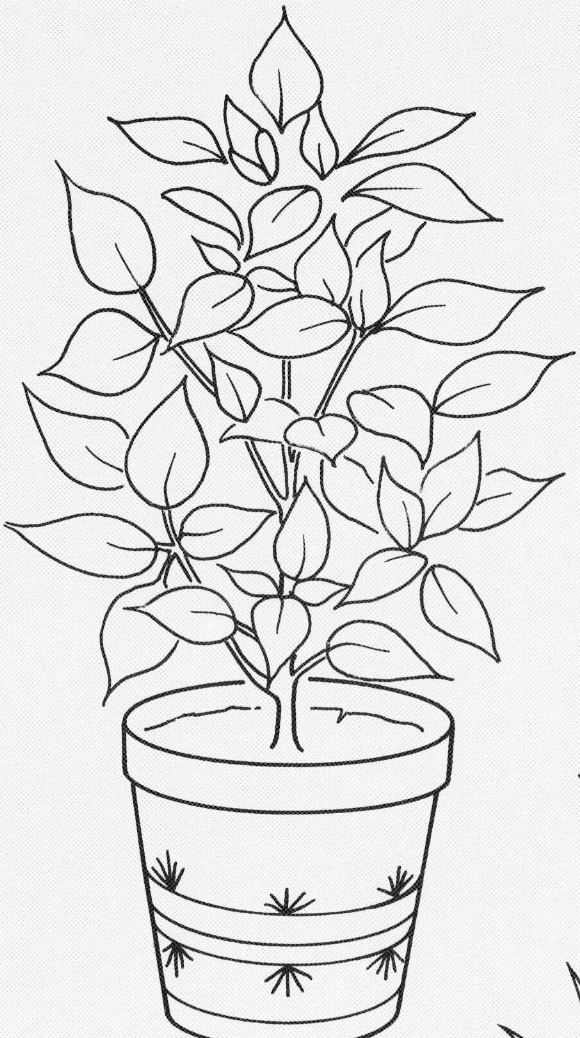

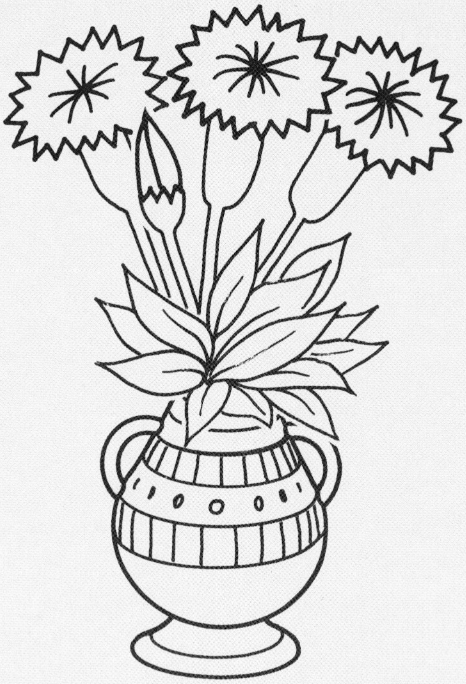

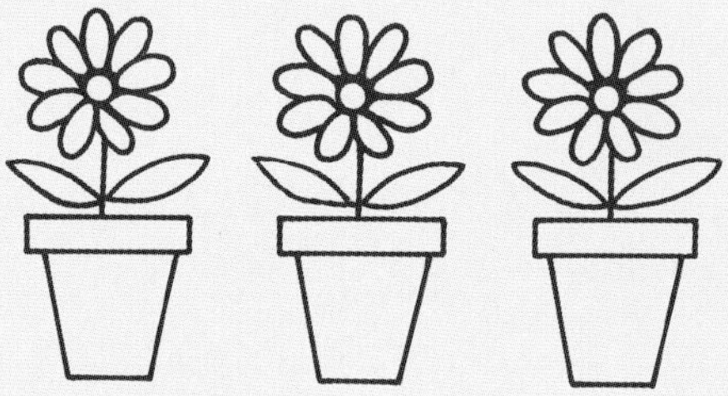

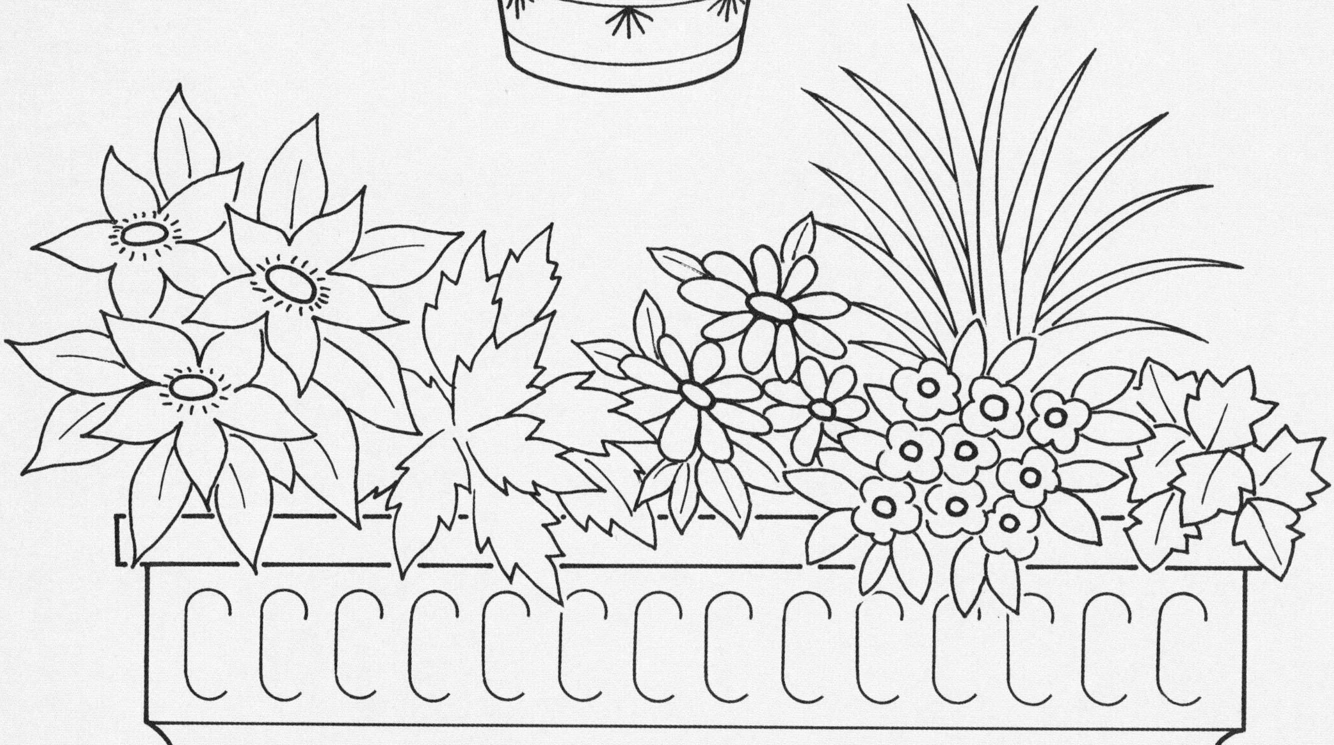

Chapter 7

GARDEN PATHS

Garden paths take their character from the materials used to construct them – bricks, flagstones, gravel, wood, crazy paving or black-and-white chequered tiles. Their outlines might be softened by creeping and spreading plants poking out between the cracks, and they can be edged by smartly clipped box hedging or pretty flowering annuals.

PREVIOUS PAGE A path leading to a sundial surrounded by beautiful summer flowers makes a delightful subject for a tent stitch picture.

The garden path was originally designed to lead you through the garden to see every corner, not just to stop you treading on the plants. My favourite is a path made from wood chips and bark scattered with wild flowers, leading through a secluded woodland area and meandering around a pond. In Japan, the path is an especially important feature of a garden, as they believe it to be an integral part of the whole garden experience. A path in a landscaped Japanese garden might change in texture as you walk along it, moving from crunchy gravel to smooth, flat stones.

Appliqué and machine embroidery are used for this flower-edged stone pathway.

The needlepoint stitches change in colour and scale to show the perspective of the path leading beneath the topiary hedges.

A wander up any path gradually reveals each part of the garden as it winds its way across the lawn to the flower beds and into the distance. Look at the shape it makes across the garden. What is the path made from? Bricks, stones, pebbles? There are so many different shapes and textures which give a path its distinctive appearance and character.

Try to look closely at the varied patterns made by the materials used for the path. They might be geometric, for example, a brick herringbone design, or completely random like crazy paving. You can make rough sketches of the designs, and use graph paper to plot any geometric shapes. You could interpret paths with regular patterns in counted thread techniques such as needlepoint or blackwork. Irregularly shaped paths might be better worked in appliqué or free-style embroidery. One simple way to embroider a path is to outline the stones or bricks using stem stitch or back stitch, filling in with satin stitch to make the design more three-dimensional.

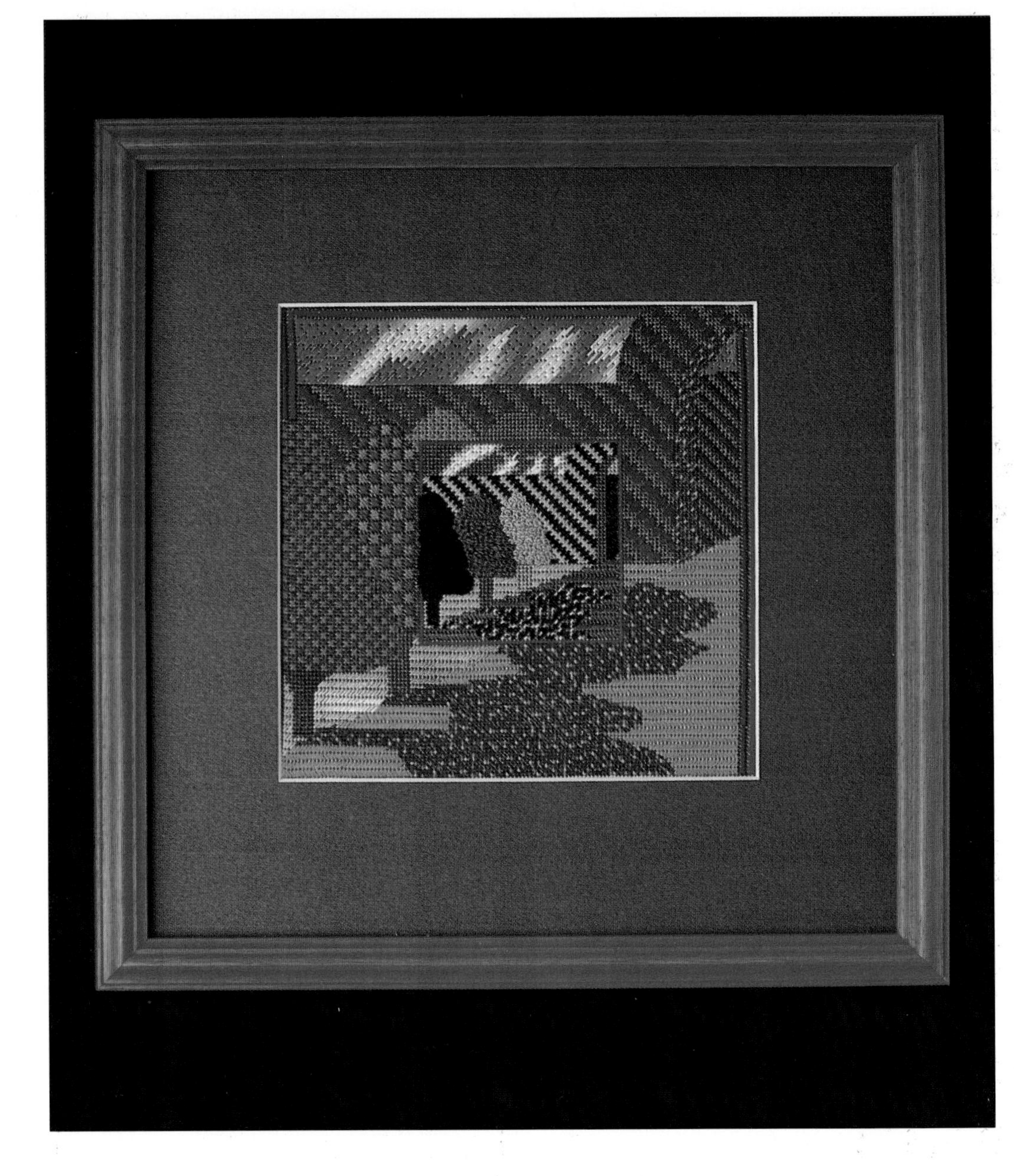

This interpretation of a pathway through a formal garden has a smaller monochrome version superimposed on top of the main picture.

Knot gardens make a wonderful subject for counted thread embroidery. The paths in a knot garden interlock in a fascinating variety of patterns, separating small formal flower or herb beds which are often surrounded by low hedges. Varying your colour scheme can produce completely different effects. Experiment with the same design, using, for instance, strongly contrasting colours in one piece and only colours which are very close in hue in another.

Smart suburban front gardens with rectangular lawns usually have simple paths, with annual edging plants spilling on to them. A design based on a path with flowers will be given extra visual interest by varying the embroidery stitches used for the plants. At different times of the year the plants and their colours will vary greatly; note these changes as they occur and record the combinations you like with photographs and small sketches. I have a straight path in my front garden, but I have planted nasturtiums and lemon balm which have grown over the path so much that you have to zigzag around them at the end of the summer. In the

spring, by contrast, it is delicately edged with snowdrops and crocuses.

Meandering pathways might lead you past a sundial or an ornate garden bench. Or they could take you under an archway or pergola, or through hedges clipped into the ornamental shapes of topiary. All these features would make interesting studies for an embroidered picture. So whether you prefer to focus on the fine detail of the textures in a path, or whether you take a wider view of the overall colour and shape, garden paths can give rise to some beautiful designs for embroidery of all kinds.

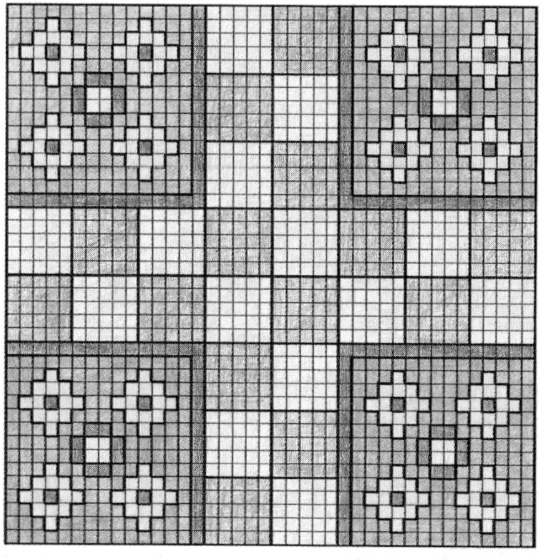

A chequerboard patterned path divides the little formal flower-beds on this pretty pincushion worked in tent stitch.

The summer house design shown on this page would make a very pretty picture in free-style embroidery. You can add features of your own such as bright flowers, birds on the path or roof, and clouds in the sky. Try to graduate the colour of your thread along the pathway and among the greenery to give a feeling of depth and perspective to your picture.

The garden path designs on these pages are just some of the many patterns to be found in gardens around the country and can create interesting and unusual ideas for your work. The charted design could be embroidered in cross stitch on to a table runner or worked in needlepoint as a purse. The other patterns could be worked in appliqué with topstitching or as effective quilted borders in self-coloured or contrasting threads.

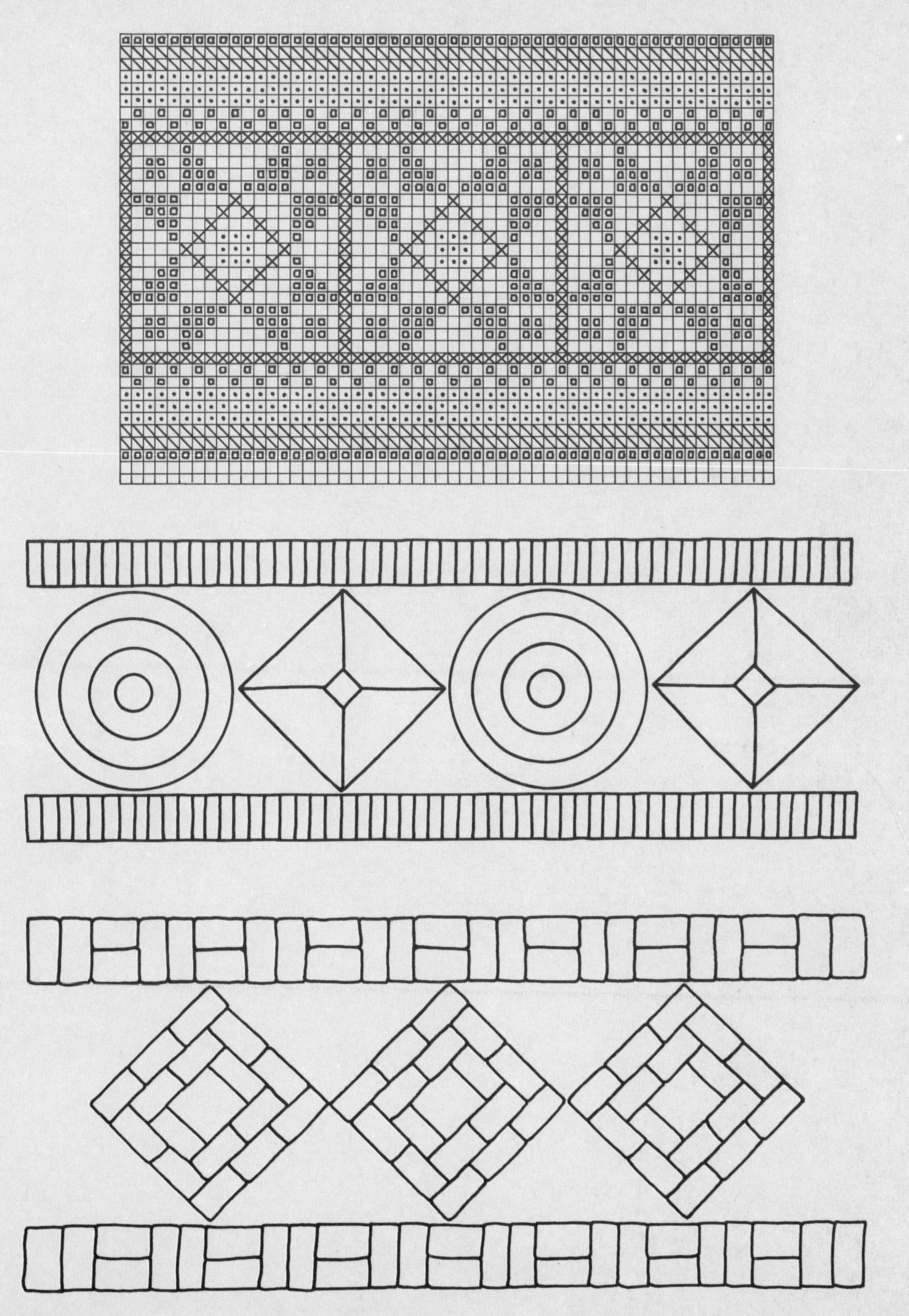

These motifs taken from garden paths and garden designs can be used in an abstract way to build up patterns in your work or as part of a realistic scene. Use a combination of thread colours and textures to suit the materials from which the path is made. The circular garden view would make a pretty picture for a hall or living room, worked in intricate detail with realistic colours. The shell design is appropriate for the bathroom, perhaps on guest towels or on individual face-cloths, using different colours for each guest. You might like to use machined appliqué for the main shape with rows of narrow machine satin stitch for the inner lines.

The path designs on the opposite page make effective abstract borders. The more regular shapes can be charted for counted thread work. The maze would make a fascinating small picture in toning shades of green. Use outline stitches for the hedges, then fill in with French knots or seeding if you wish.

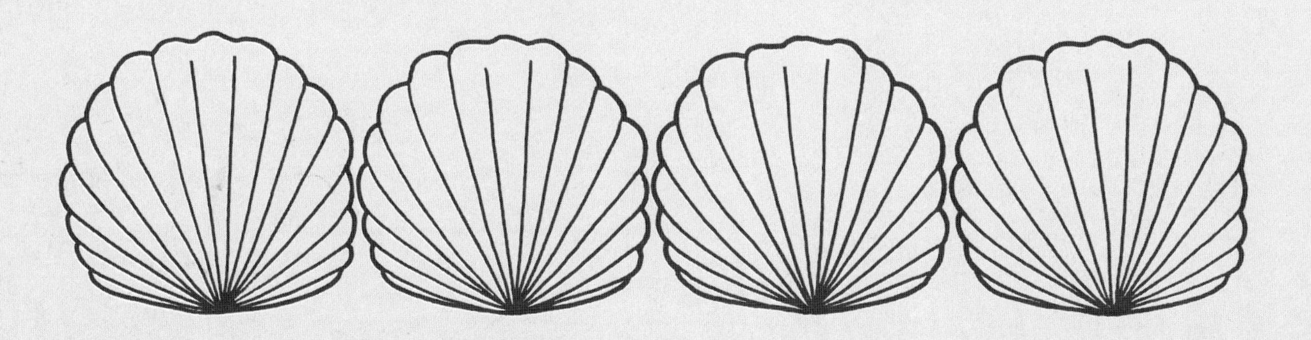

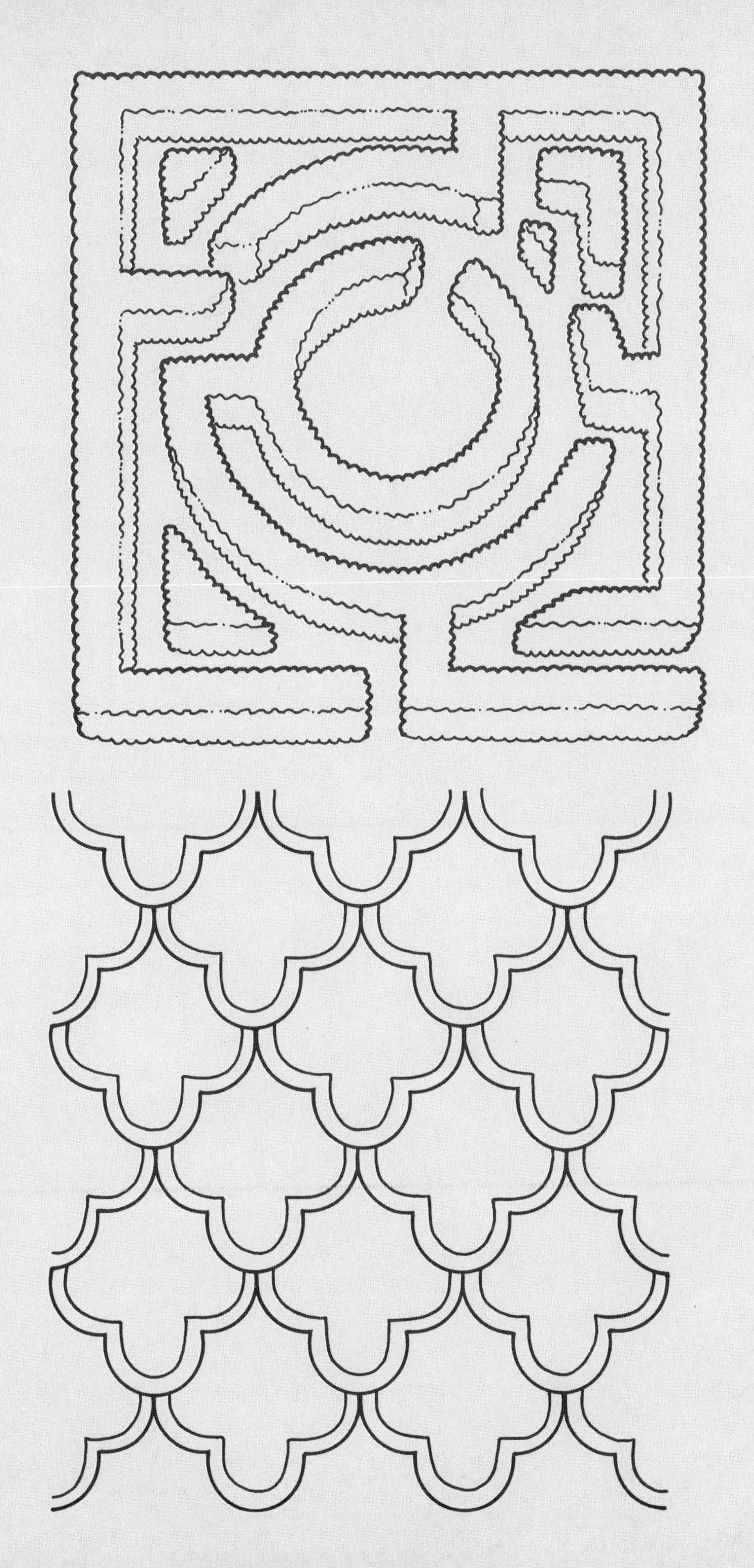

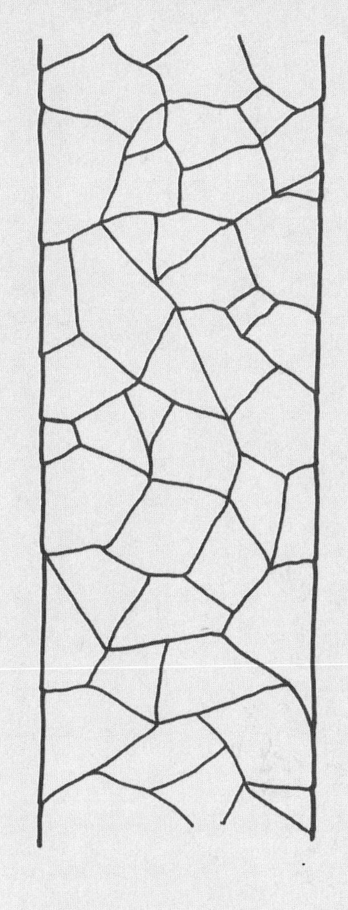

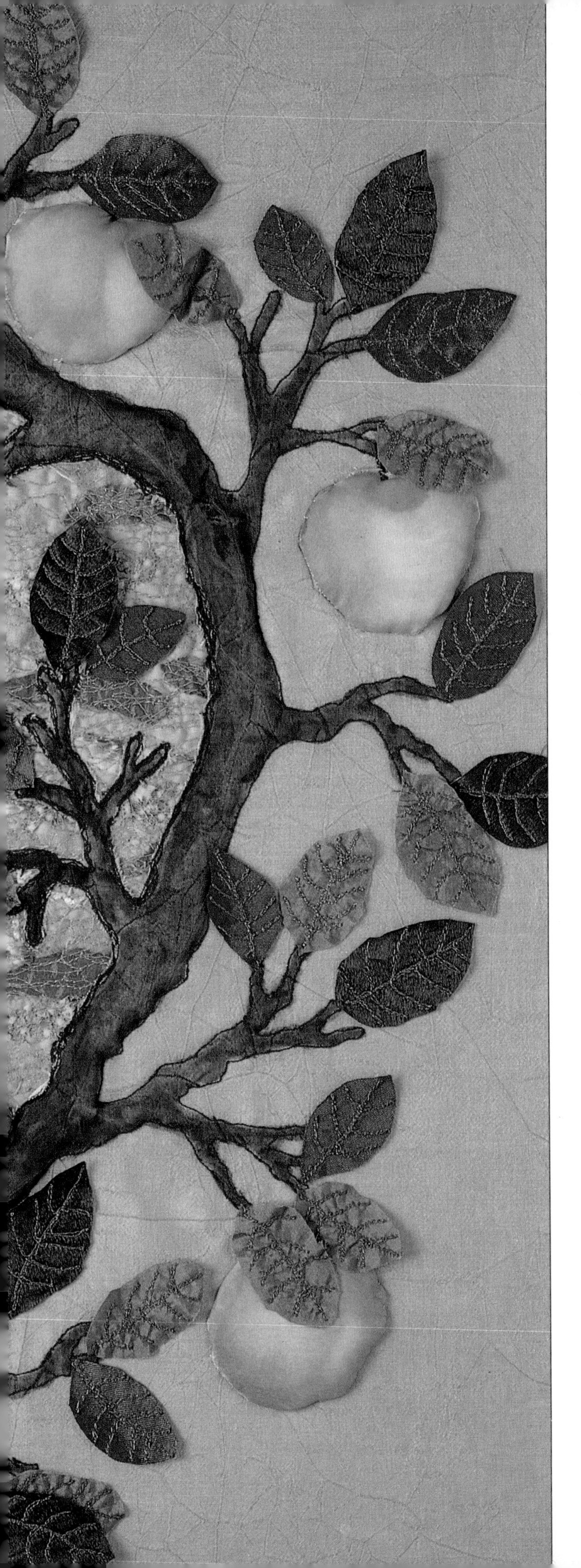

Chapter 8

KITCHEN GARDENS

Out in the kitchen garden plump fruit ripens in the sun and rows of vegetables burst out of the soil. Fruit and vegetables make wonderful subjects for embroidered items which can be put to a variety of uses, especially around the kitchen. Quilted pot stands and beautifully stitched tablecloths, tea towels or aprons make special gifts for the clever cook who turns the garden produce into the food we eat.

PREVIOUS PAGE *Appliqué and machine embroidery are combined in this lyrical design of a thrush in an apple tree.*

As I walk up my garden, I am filled with a feeling of anticipation and excitement as I reach the patch at the end where I grow my vegetables and fruit. I can't wait to see how much they have grown since I last saw them. Nothing gives me as a gardener quite the sense of pride that home produce does. This makes interpreting kitchen garden designs especially enjoyable for me.

The stylized forms of ordinary fruit, vegetable and leaf shapes make wonderful counted thread designs. You could cross-stitch them around the yoke and collar of a peasant-style blouse, or around the cuffs and hem of a warm winter cardigan. Fruit and vegetables can be used just as effectively for free-style embroidery, and for appliqué and quilting designs.

RIGHT *A lavish display of flowers and produce in a greenhouse is interpreted in appliqué with machine embroidery and some hand stitching.*

ABOVE *Simple running stitch has been used to great effect in this detail of garden vegetables.*

The different textures in this design of a corner of the kitchen garden are created with dyed calico, hand embroidery in stranded cotton and wooden bean poles.

I love the contrast in the colours of fruit and vegetables, from the vibrant reds of tomatoes and juicy cherries to the earthy oranges and browns of the root crops. You could choose a fruit or vegetable from each season, from spring greens to autumn berries, and stitch a small needlepoint kneeling cushion backed with leather for the gardener in your family. Or make a beautiful tablecloth with summer fruits and flowers embroidered on to it to cheer you up in the winter. You don't have to worry about how realistic your drawings are. Simple shapes stitched in flat bright colours are sometimes just as appealing as more sophisticated work and are ideal for children's designs in the nursery or playroom, or as motifs for appliqué or quilting.

This bold, beautifully constructed design of a bird in the vineyard is worked in the unusual technique of felt inlay.

This delightful alphabet sampler features a repeat design of a country cottage with its flower, fruit and vegetable gardens. It is worked entirely by hand, using a variety of free-style embroidery stitches.

A wonderful way to find inspiration is to visit the shops in your local town which sell unusual imported vegetables and fruit for the different communities in your area. Some of the things you might find are chillies, okra, fresh figs, sharon fruit, yams and plantain, which can be embroidered individually or in groups on to everyday items around your own home.

If you live in a country which has vegetables like these freely available, you might find the humble English cabbage interesting. A great way to interpret a cabbage design is to cut the cabbage cleanly in half and lay it flat side down on a photocopier. The photocopied image can then be traced off and used as a pattern. Red cabbages are very good for this as the contrast between the red and white of the leaves is so marked. The insides of sliced peppers or mushrooms also show interesting patterns which can easily be

The simplest designs can look very effective. Here, an apple motif has been appliquéd on to the corner of a napkin.

interpreted in a variety of stitches with areas of texture worked with French knots and wooden beads.

Fruit trees in the garden provide different colours and shapes for embroiderers throughout the year, from stark bare branches in winter to frothy pink and white blossom in spring and heavy fruit in late summer and early autumn. An orchard scene would make a colourful embroidered picture for a kitchen or conservatory, and could be worked in needlepoint, cross stitch or free-style embroidery.

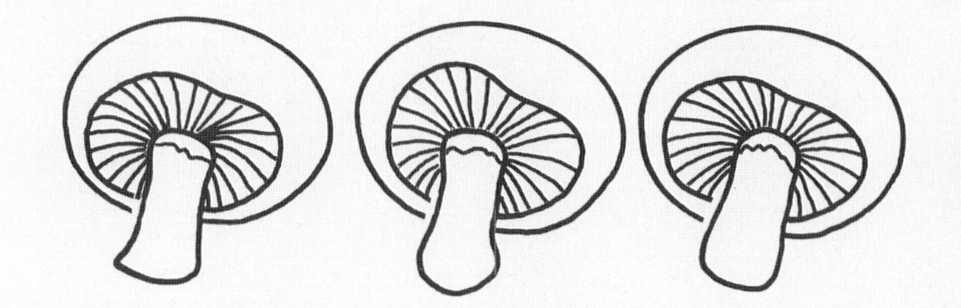

Use the motifs on these pages to brighten up your kitchen. Try stitching some lettuce leaf oven gloves in shades of green; these simple outlines make very effective designs. A border of tomatoes or mushrooms can be stitched along the edge of a tea towel or a kitchen place mat, or could even make a shelf edging with a difference. Strawberry-field curtains can easily be created by embroidering a row of fruit along the bottom near the hem or by dotting the strawberries about in a random way across the material. For fun, you could use a mixture of motifs to make your own fruit salad. The runner bean design on the opposite page would look effective climbing up the front of an apron made from a heavy cotton fabric in a natural colour – a lovely present to give an enthusiastic gardener friend.

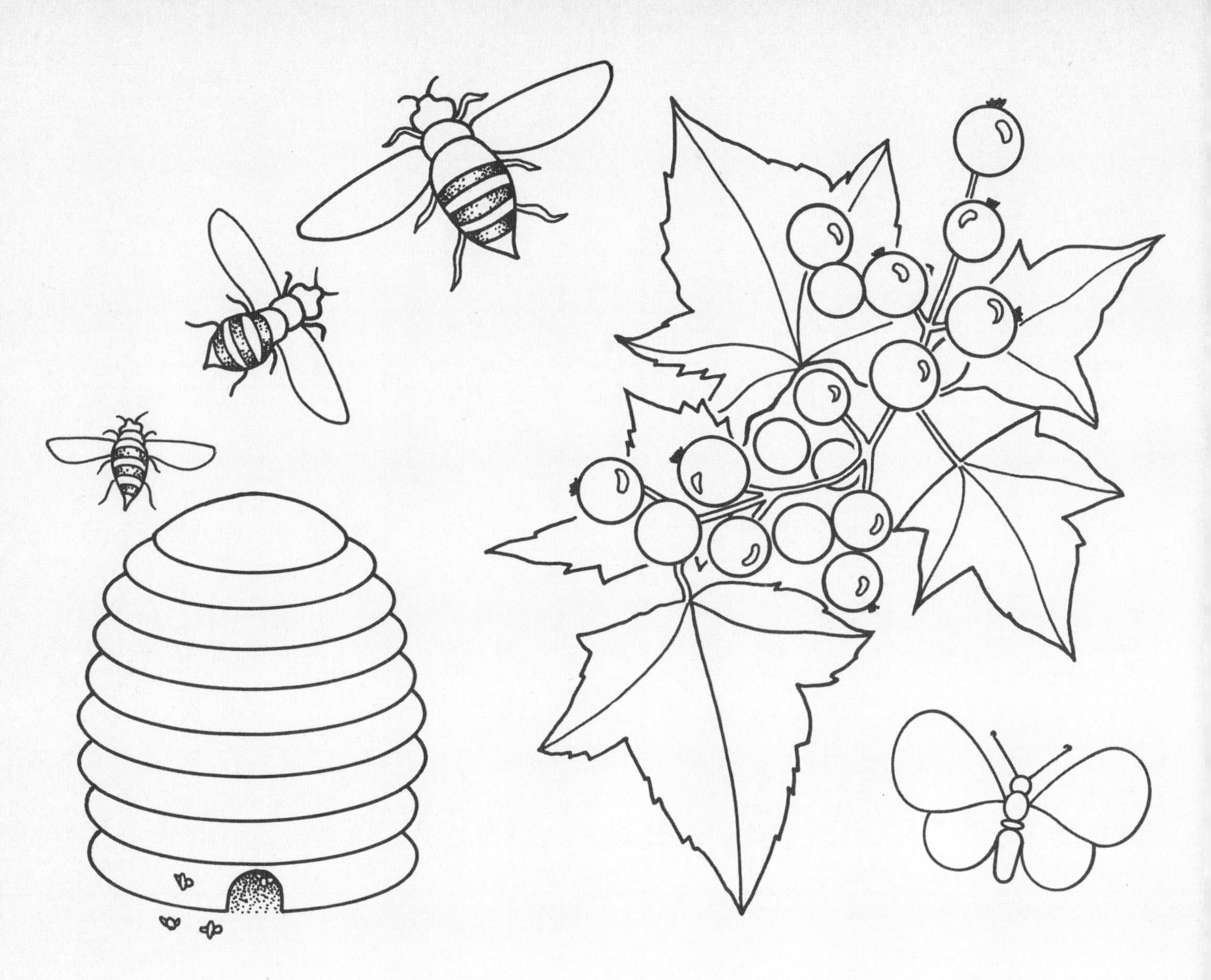

The bumble bees on these pages are appealing motifs for kitchen items, accessories or children's clothes. The charted cherry design could be worked in cross stitch over waste canvas on to a simple apron or a tee-shirt. The blackberry or currant designs work well on table linen such as a cloth or mat, and you can interpret them in a variety of stitches. You might like to select part of the design such as a leaf and flowers, or berries and flowers to repeat on a set of napkins.

These motifs can be used all around the home, but are especially appropriate in the kitchen, dining room and conservatory. The panel on the opposite page would work very well in long-and-short stitch with the details added in back stitch, stem stitch and French knots. If enlarged, it would make a wonderfully colourful piece of appliqué, again with embroidered details. Try appliqué, too, for the simple, bold fruit design at the bottom of this page. It would translate well into bright primary colours on a child's summer tee-shirt or the back of a denim jacket.

The figs would lend themselves to crewel work in wool, or they could be drawn on to canvas for a rich needlepoint piece. The dill, on the other hand, is a delicate pattern which is best suited to free-style embroidery in fine threads, perhaps on a herb bag.

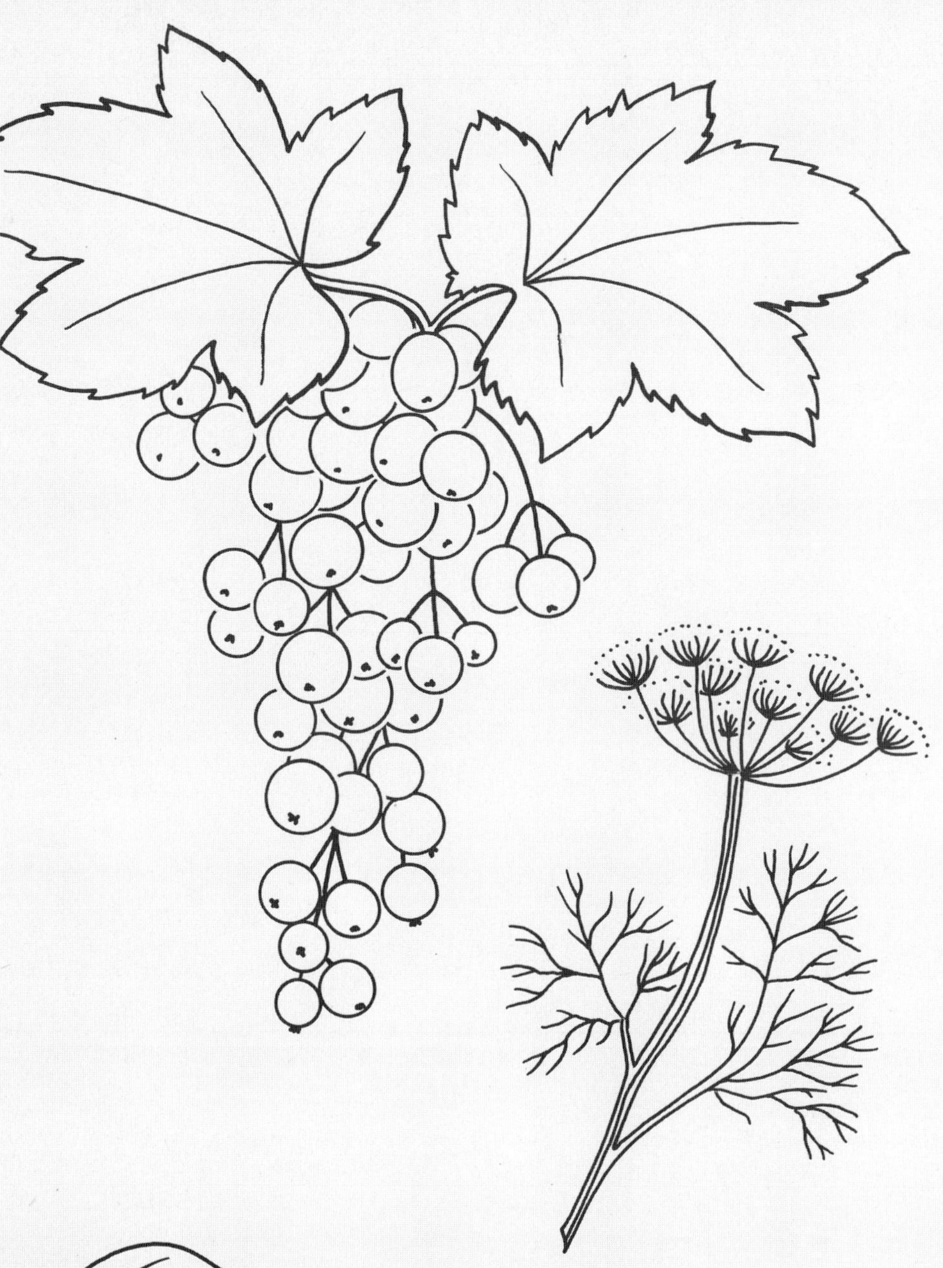

Chapter 9

FLOWER GARDENS

Cultivated flowers have been a source of inspiration for embroiderers since the very first samplers were sewn. From dainty spring flowers and the glorious blooms of summer to chrysanthemums and Christmas roses, flowers can be found in the garden all year round and give endless ideas for embroidery designs.

PREVIOUS PAGE Flowers grow in profusion over this stunning quilted hanging which incorporates appliqué, hand-painting and embroidery.

BELOW This abstract flower design in machine and hand embroidery has beads added for texture.

Flowers and foliage have always been among the most versatile and widely used motifs. Time after time they lend just the right touch to embroidered items, whether in counted thread or free-style work. Flower designs make lovely gifts for all occasions, such as birthdays, birth celebrations or anniversaries. A lovely idea is to use the favourite flower of the person for whom the gift is intended. For a new baby you could choose a flower that blooms in the month in which the baby was born. A personalized gift is always extra special.

Flowers can bring a light summery feel to any room and make an ideal project for a beginner. A rose-bud in simple cross stitch could be easily tackled. Bring the garden into the living room by embroidering cushion covers for a chair, tie-backs for curtains or a fire-screen for a fireplace. In the bedroom, pale mauve wistaria or lilac, delicate forget-me-nots or an elegant rose embroidered on to pillow cases and sheets would add a romantic touch. Embroidered bed linen is a particularly nice gift, and plain white cotton sheets and pillowcases can be bought quite cheaply or made from sheeting fabric sold in extra-wide widths.

As well as focusing on individual flowers, why not embroider a picture of a complete garden scene with herbaceous borders or formal beds. This could be a realistic view like the one opposite, or an impressionistic interpretation in blocks of colours. With flowers, the scope is endless.

RIGHT This sensitive three-dimensional portrayal of tulips has been created using a variety of techniques – fabric painting, quilting, machine embroidery and appliqué.

OPPOSITE French knots, detached chain stitch and long-and-short stitch are among the free-style embroidery stitches used in this picture of an idyllic country garden.

Floral designs are perfect to use all around the home. This camellia motif on a towel has been worked in simple embroidery stitches such as buttonhole stitch, running stitch, satin stitch and stem stitch.

Flowers make perfect designs for weddings. You could embroider simple headbands or sashes for small bridesmaids, while a more ambitious project would be to embroider the bodice of a wedding dress, matching the flowers which are to be used in the bride's bouquet. Using a chain stitch in white silk, you could embroider around the edge of the net veil with a small looped design, adding a tiny pearl or sequin where the loops cross over. After the big day a cross stitch floral frame for a special photograph makes a touching and lasting gift for the couple.

I especially love flower designs because you can sew with many different types of threads in a multitude of colours for the petals and leaves. Using fresh greens and yellows at the beginning of the year, clear blues, pinks and

This cheerful needlepoint picture of pansies is a simple enough project for a beginner to work.

whites for the summer, oranges and browns in autumn and rich reds and deep greens for winter, with flowers you can truly reflect the seasons all around your home.

If you don't have easy access to a garden, gardening books and seed catalogues are ideal for finding designs. The colour photographs in them can easily be copied or traced off. Libraries sometimes have charming old gardening encyclopedias which are full of colour and black-and-white illustrations. Or visit your local garden centre where the displays of flowers can be photographed and sketched. Here you will also find a large range of seeds in colourfully designed packets that can be adapted for embroidery motifs.

This selection of floral designs caters for all tastes. The border patterns would look delightful worked around collars, cuffs and hemlines. The Scottish thistles would also look lovely embroidered with woollen thread on to a winter cardigan.

The flower design above was sketched from some old china in a friend's kitchen, while the border design at the bottom of this page was taken from an Arabian bowl. This pattern could easily be embroidered in silky threads down either side of the button band or along the yoke of a blouse to give an Eastern feel to the garment. The bouquet, embroidered in white stranded cotton, would add something special to a plain white nightdress, and the elegant rose in cross stitch is a classic that can be used again and again on different items.

Floral designs brighten up clothing such as skirts, blouses and summer dresses. They also have unlimited uses around the home, and on accessories such as bags and belts. You might like to try a combination of fabric paint and embroidery or appliqué to vary your work, and you could add beads and sequins for texture. The simpler flower outlines could be quilted.

The daisy ring design would really cheer up plain seat covers for garden or conservatory furniture. The simple floral border on the left could be worked by a child, using felt appliqué with simple stitches such as stem stitch and detached chain stitch. For an easy needlepoint project, try drawing the little sprig of flowers opposite onto canvas with a waterproof pen and then filling in the design with tent stitch for a pretty pincushion.

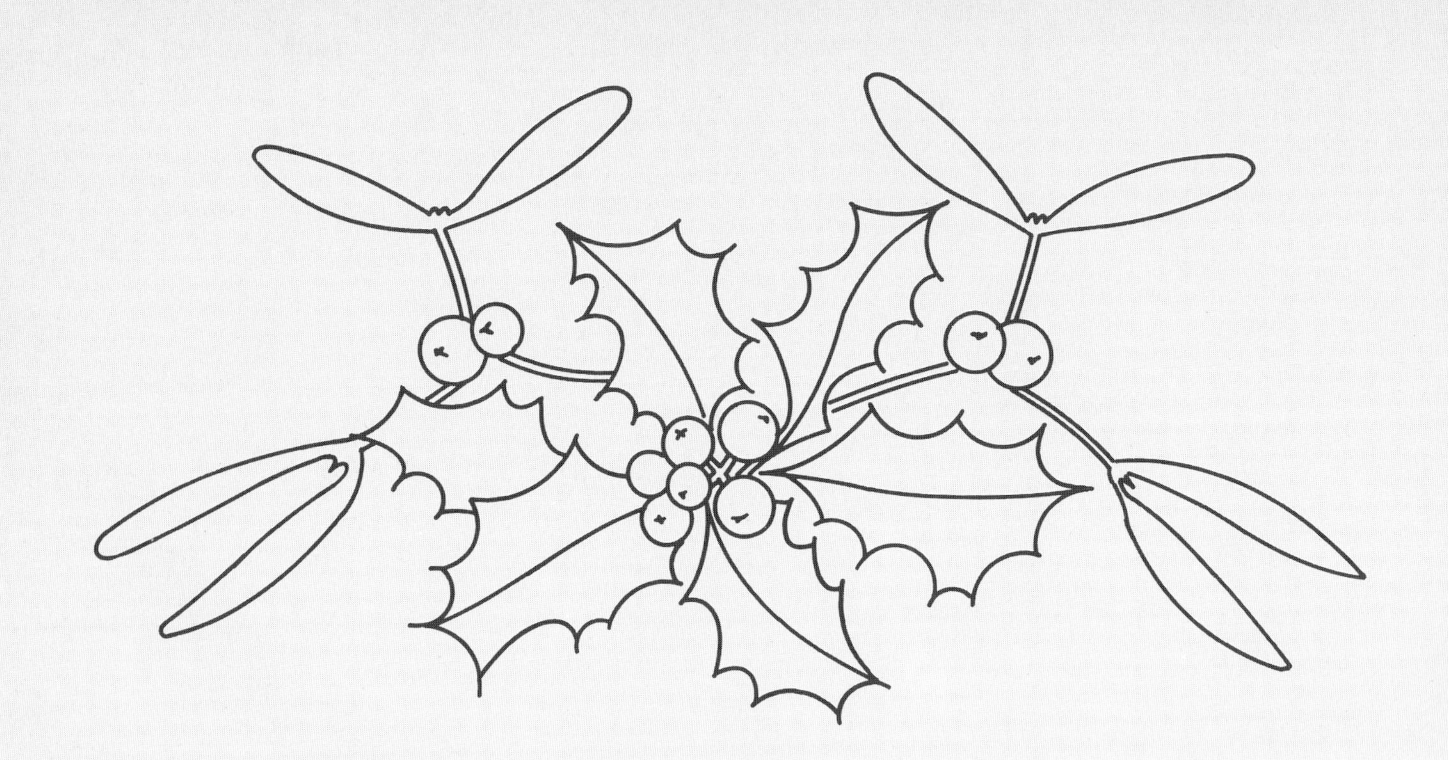

Decorate countless items with these flower designs. The repeat pattern of the snowdrops would be very pretty running around the hem of a plain gathered skirt and the single daisy motif can be repeated at random in simple stitches across a cotton sweater. The holly and mistletoe would bring a seasonal feel to a hat and gloves set.

The large border design on the opposite page could make a stunning picture frame or photograph frame in free-style embroidery. Or work the cross-stitch design around a small linen tablecloth, repeating the pattern on matching napkins. For another project, the cross stitch design could be stitched on to an evenweave band which is then applied as a border to a pair of curtains.

Chapter 10

GATES, FENCES AND WALLS

A romantic ornamental gate leading into a garden is so much more than just a practical object. Gates, fences and walls are designed in many different ways – huge and forbidding, small and elegant or purely decorative. The style and colour often reflect the house behind, from the grandest manor to the humblest country cottage.

PREVIOUS PAGE This imposing gate is part of a large needlepoint picture of a grand walled garden.

The word gate comes from the old English word *gaet* meaning a portcullis or drawbridge in a city wall. As life became more peaceful and generally safer, the gate and wall became more decorative. Grand country manor houses had elaborate and beautiful wrought-iron gates and stone walls, many of which can still be seen around the countryside.

Today, gates, fences and walls are designed to allow the passer-by a view of the house and garden while still defining the perimeter. I love peeping through a pretty gate into a lovely garden. Sometimes a garden design

This picture of an archway in an old brick wall is interpreted realistically with applied fabrics and both hand and machine embroidery.

incorporates this romantic idea. A gate may be placed mid-way along a garden, so that a person approaching it can look through with anticipation before opening it and walking into the next section of the garden.

Some of the most attractive designs may be close to your own home, so you will not have to go far to find them. While researching this book, much to my amazement, I found a lovely gate a few doors from my own house, which I had been walking past for two years and not noticed!

ABOVE *The white painted wooden gate is the central feature of this scene worked in tent stitch.*

ABOVE LEFT *Several different needlepoint stitches add interest to this charming picture of a country gateway.*

LEFT *This composition of flowers in front of a garden fence employs various techniques – appliqué, machine embroidery and fabric painting.*

Draw small sketches of the gates and fences that you like. When you are looking for inspiration for embroidery, you can use your sketches as a starting point, and then arrange them in an abstract way or in rows to create borders which can be extended and repeated to run right around the edge of a tablecloth or the hem of a skirt, for example.

To make a design symmetrical, trace half of it on to a sheet of tracing paper, then retrace the design, turning the paper over to draw the other side. You can draw around coins or glasses to make curves, and graph paper or lined paper will help you to keep your spacing correct.

A variety of embroidery techniques can be used for different designs. Fences and railings have a regular geometric simplicity, ideal for counted thread work such as Assisi work, cross stitch or needlepoint. By contrast, a

The detail on the stone wall in the foreground of this charming view is simply stitched, but works very effectively.

wrought-iron gate could be portrayed in couching, stem stitch or split stitch, and a wall in appliqué or quilting, with fabric paint for texture.

Your imagination can run away with you when planning an embroidered picture. Once you have stitched the basic gate, fence or wall shape, you can adorn it with all kinds of foliage, drape it with flowering clematis or other climbing plant, or add box hedging peeping over the top. You can also bring this kind of design to life by adding a cat or dog, a bird or even neighbours chatting over the wall!

Assisi work has been used in this design to outline the railings and to fill in the flowering shrubs behind them. Ordinary cross stitch, or a variation of it, can be used for the flowers.

Beautiful wrought iron gates can be used in an abstract way to form a repeated pattern or border. Enlarge the images on a photocopier and use the whole design or just a section of it to repeat as you wish in colours that you wouldn't normally associate with gates! Alternatively, you may want to try and place a gate into a composition of your own, including designs from other chapters. The stone archway design opposite, with its scrambling flowers, will give you plenty of scope to use a lot of stitch variations. Try using beads, too, and different thicknesses of thread to add texture to your design.

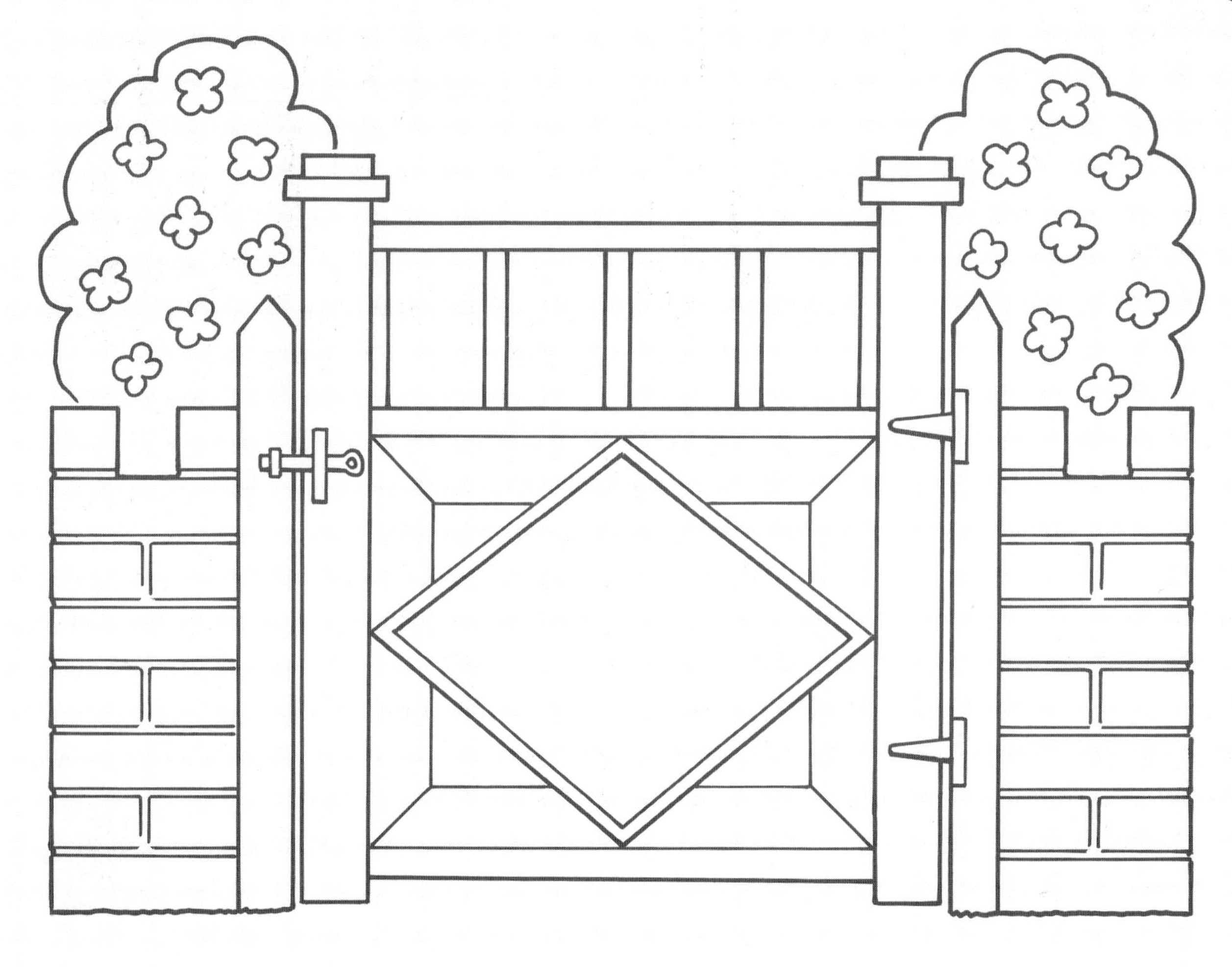

Use these gates as designs on their own or place them in the foreground of garden compositions to build up a complete picture. The gate design at the bottom of the opposite page would work well enlarged and used in an abstract way. The picket fence and gate shown opposite could have different types of greenery growing behind it and peeping through it to make a realistic picture. One of the sweet little dogs can be placed in front of a gate to add a humorous touch, and they are also fun to use on children's clothes such as dungarees, blouses and tee-shirts.

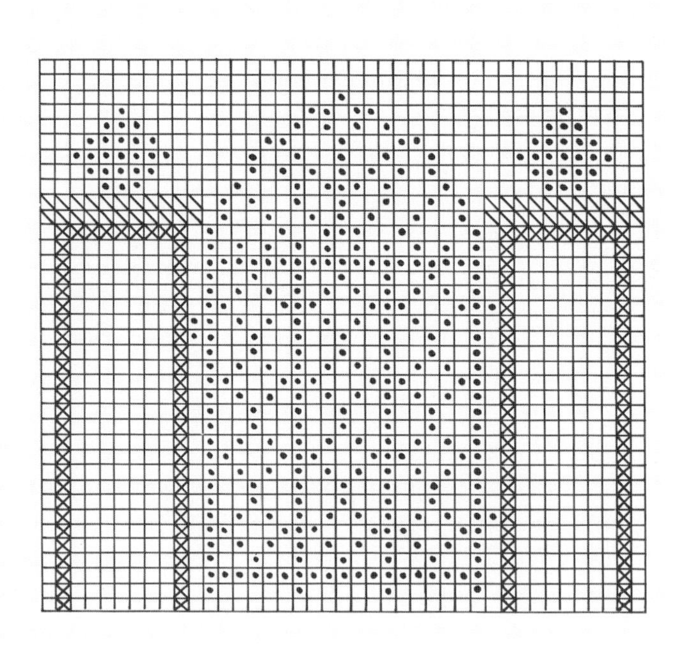

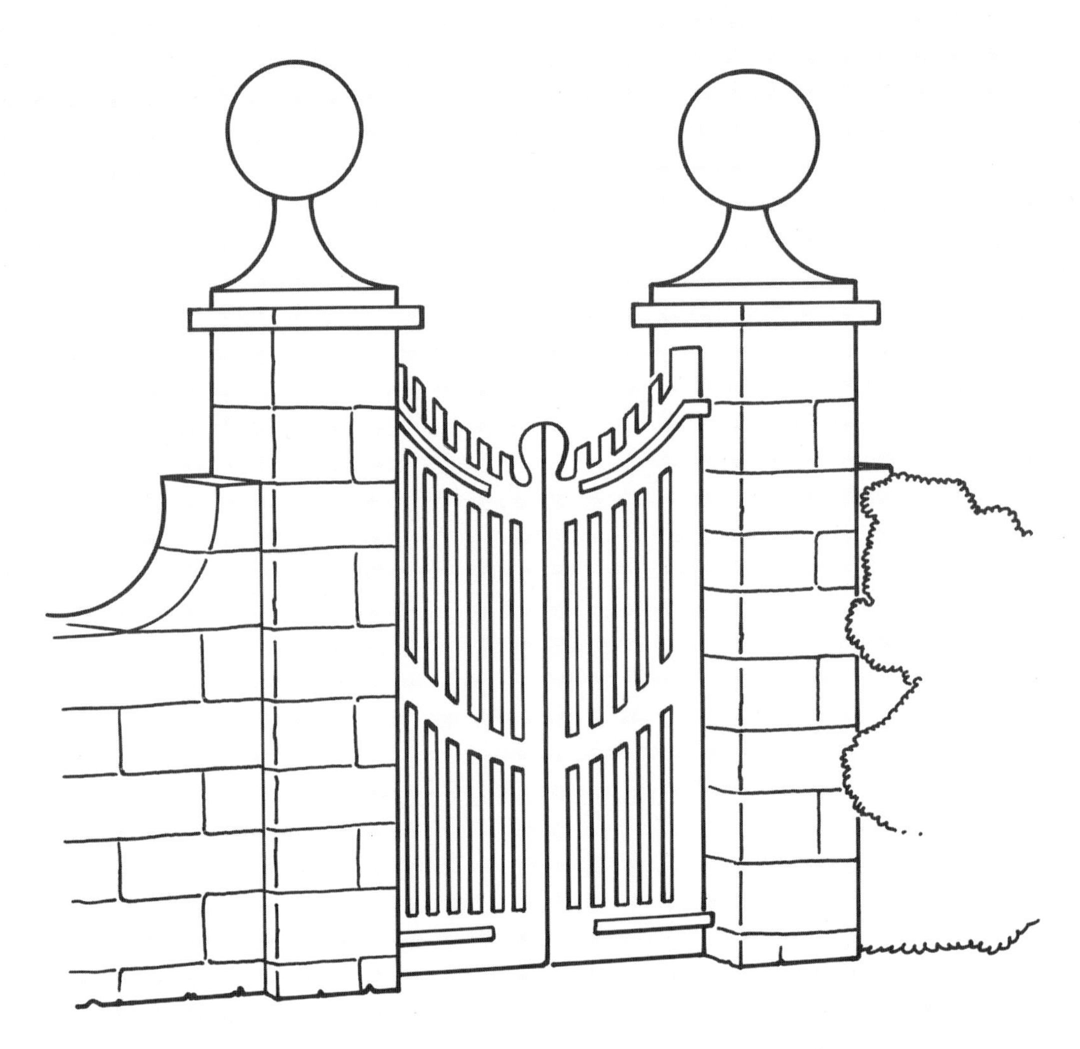

Chapter 11

PONDS AND FOUNTAINS

It is said that no garden is complete without some form of water, and certainly nothing quite compares to the beauty of an ornate stone fountain and the sound of water spraying high into the air. Just as delightful is a trickling stream, flowing into a pond teaming with life. Frogs, goldfish and water-lilies are all shapes which can be outlined very simply and worked as borders or as individual motifs.

PREVIOUS PAGE A peaceful corner of a garden, with a small pond surrounded by crazy paving and beautiful flowers, makes a lovely subject for a needlepoint picture.

I am always fascinated by garden ponds, whether they are formal with a stone wall surround and a fountain or more natural with curved edges and a few water plants. You never quite know what lurks in the murky depths: goldfish hiding under the lily pads or a frog sitting so still that you don't notice him until, plop, he leaps into the water!

To bring a natural feeling to your work, try using unusual materials or found objects such as straw and raffia, or leaves and pieces of bark for the background to a pond design. You could make holes in small seeds and use them as beads in your design. Thin twigs could add a extra dimension to the piece and fluffy feathers could represent high grasses around the pond's edge. Working on to silk and satin will give a shiny watery feel. Add green leather for lily pad leaves and coarse woollen thread for rushes to make a dramatic textural combination.

Reflections in water make an interesting subject to embroider. A layer of fine gauze or coloured net laid over the embroidery stitches which represent the water of a pond will give an impression of hazy reflected shapes. Alternatively, you could change the shades of the threads very slightly for the reflections, or stitch over fabric paint in watery-looking colours.

The pond in this landscaped garden is worked in long stitch on a canvas background.

Dyed calico, layers of net, beads and hand embroidery in stranded cotton are used to create texture in this picture of a pond showing the reflections of the shrubs around it.

Fish glinting beneath the surface of the water add a splash of golden colour to this close-up design of a pond worked in appliqué and machine embroidery.

Ponds and fountains are appropriate motifs for items in the bathroom as blues and greens make lovely bathroom colours. A cluster of water-lilies, their creamy petals tinged with pink or yellow, could be embroidered on to a pale blue towel to make a charming addition to anyone's bathroom. The same motif stitched on to a silky wrap, using a combination of thread and fabric paint to show the ripples on the water, would make a charming gift for someone special.

Fountains make beautiful arched patterns; working the stitches gradually smaller as the droplets of water fall will give a sense of perspective. Silver thread will give the impression of light sparkling on the water, and tiny pearl beads can be incorporated into the design. Sculpted stone bases with mermaids, cherubs and fishes can be stitched in a variety of threads in shades of grey, or worked in appliqué with stitching on top.

A stylized design of an ornate fountain makes an unusual motif for a cross-stitch spectacles case.

Of all the wildlife found in and around a pond, dragonflies are my favourite. I love the way they hover for a moment in the sun, the movement of their iridescent wings barely detectable and their colours so beautiful that they take your breath away. Worked in silk as a tiny design in gleaming turquoise blues and greens, a dragonfly would add a really special touch to a white blouse. You could use scraps of shiny satin or silk and silver thread for its wings, combined with fabric paint on the body to bring it to life.

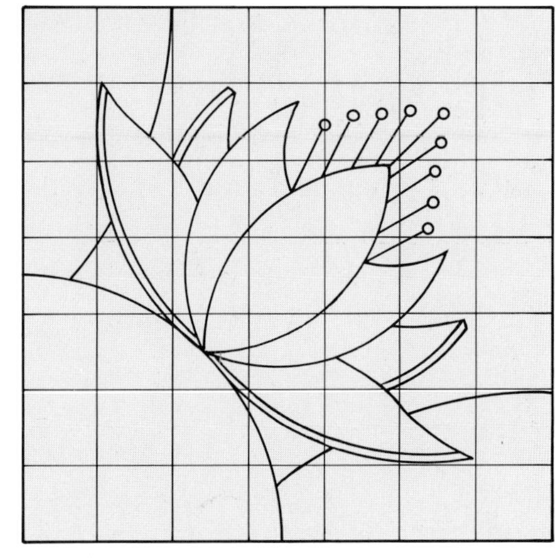

This sumptuous satin cushion in machine appliqué uses a bold water-lily design as a repeated corner motif.

Use these motifs inspired by pond life to brighten up your bathroom or beach wear. Embroider a green frog in the corner of bathroom curtains or run a row of tiny fish all along the edge of a towel. The bulrushes remind me of my childhood expeditions to local ponds. Work the leaves in dull greens and use shades of brown wool for realistic bulrush heads.

The angel fish cross-stitch design could be worked over waste canvas on to bath robes, beach towels and bags. As it is a tropical fish, don't be afraid to use really vivid colours. The fountain and pond could be used as a centrepiece in a garden composition, but it would look exquisite as a picture in its own right, worked in free-style embroidery, with fine silver threads for the falling drops of water.

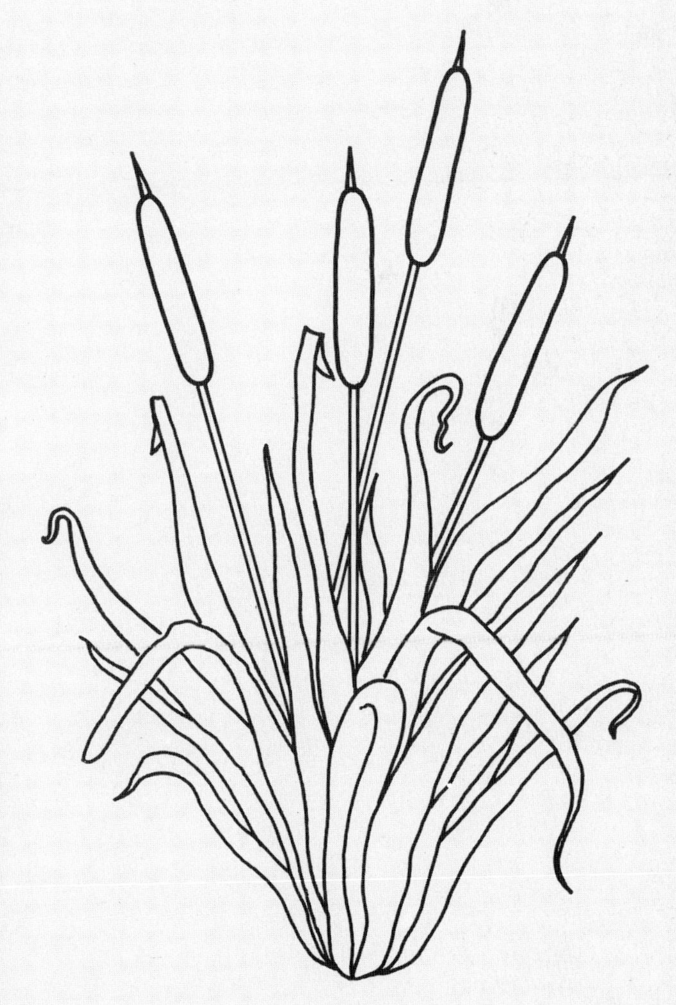

There is plenty of scope to use your own favourite stitch variations for these pond motifs. Try adding reflective materials such as glass beads and shiny satin to give your work a 'watery' feel. The water-lilies and the jumping fish are perfect subjects for appliqué with stitched details. Fabric paints come into their own with waterlife motifs, too. The stencil-like fish designs can be painted first, and then outlined or further embellished with fine embroidery stitches. The duck would be the perfect finishing touch to a child's dungarees or rompers.

The waterlife panel shown opposite would make a beautiful bell-pull. You would need to enlarge the design and transfer it onto a firmly woven linen or cotton fabric, then bring it to life with a variety of embroidery stitches. Or you could draw the outlines onto canvas with a waterproof pen and work the design in needlepoint. Add decorative bell-pull ends at top and bottom for a neat-looking finish.

The ornate fountains on these pages can make very stylish embroidery. Silver and white thread used together will bring the authentic feel of splashing water to your work. Try stitching the base of the fountain in several different shades of grey. You might like to work the base in satin stitch, outlining the different decorative areas in back stitch, split stitch or couching.

Dragonflies in beautiful shades of turquoise and blue flying at random across a silk blouse would add a glamorous touch. Another idea is to stitch the dragonflies in shadow work across a pair of plain white voile curtains in a sunny room.

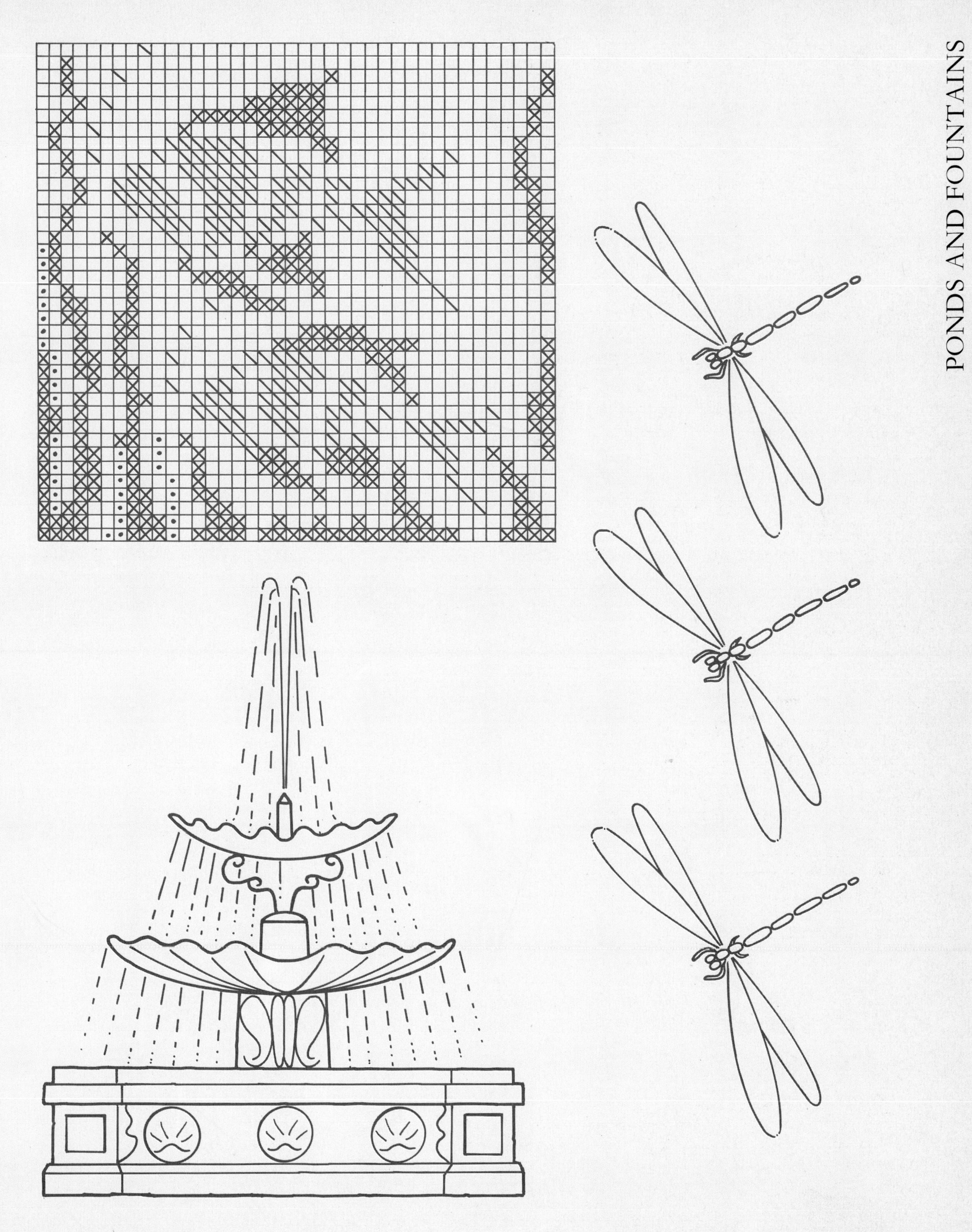

MATERIALS, TECHNIQUES AND STITCHES

This view of the sunken garden at Hampton Court Palace near London is beautifully worked in free-style embroidery.

PLANNING YOUR EMBROIDERY

Before you embark on any piece of embroidery, whether in free stitching, counted thread work, appliqué or quilting, take time to do some basic planning. Think about the feeling you are trying to create in your design and the use to which your work will be put. Then look at all the possible colours, fabrics and stitches you could use to achieve this.

This stage is always the most enjoyable for me: researching, planning alternatives and developing ideas before deciding on the final interpretation. My advice would be to follow your own instincts for each of your embroideries. In this way you will build on your own preferences and strengths, and gain in understanding with each piece of work you do.

The following guide-lines will help you with your planning and familiarize you with some of the materials, techniques and stitches you can use.

MATERIALS

THREADS There are many different types of embroidery thread in a huge range of colours, so do experiment with them instead of playing safe with just one or two familiar ones. Shiny threads include pearl cotton, coton à broder, pure silk and stranded cotton. The latter is very versatile as it can be split up into separate strands and recombined to make different thicknesses. Different shades can be mixed in this way for subtle effects.

Soft embroidery cotton is a matt thread, slightly thicker than stranded cotton. There are also some beautiful metallic threads to add sparkle to your embroidery. Woollen yarns include tapestry wool, Persian wool and crewel wool, and textured knitting wool can often give interesting effects for a change.

FABRICS Free-style embroidery can be worked on all kinds of fabric, depending on the effect you want to achieve. Cotton and linen are ideal for garments or household items, providing an excellent base for embroidery. Silk is wonderful to work with and very luxurious. Oddments of dress or furnishing fabrics can make interesting backgrounds, and calico, being inexpensive, is useful for experimenting with different stitches.

For cross stitch work, you will need evenweave fabric with easily countable threads, while, for needlepoint, canvas is available in a range of mesh sizes.

NOTIONS You can make use of some of the notions available from haberdashery departments or craft shops to add interest to your embroidery. Beads, sequins, buttons, ribbons, lace, cord and braid can all be incorporated into a design to great effect, giving it texture and detail.

A family tree with a difference – this decorative picture displays the initials of the family members on the oranges growing on the stylized needlepoint tree.

FABRIC PAINTS AND CRAYONS These add an extra dimension to an embroidery and are used by many designers to create subtle effects in their work. A painted fabric background can provide a coloured base for embroidery stitches which would be difficult to achieve in any other way.

There are paints and crayons available for use on both natural and synthetic fabrics. Depending on the type, these fabric colours can be applied with a brush, stencilled or sprayed on to fabric, or a design can be drawn on to paper and then transferred to the fabric by ironing.

EQUIPMENT

NEEDLES It is important to choose the correct type and size of needle for your work. Crewel needles have a long eye which will take various thicknesses of thread. Sharps are shorter with a smaller eye, suitable for only one or two strands of stranded cotton or for sewing thread. Betweens are short, sharp needles used in quilting. Tapestry needles are blunt and so do not split the threads of the fabric. They are used for needlepoint and cross stitch.

SCISSORS You will need a good pair of sharp pointed embroidery scissors for cutting threads and a pair of dressmaking shears for cutting fabric.

FRAMES Although some people prefer not to use a frame, it is important for many types of embroidery to work on stretched fabric. Both round and rectangular frames can be mounted on stands, leaving both hands free for stitching.

Ring frames are suitable for small areas of work and come in a range of diameters. It is a good idea to wrap a strip of thin fabric around the inner ring to protect the fabric on which you are working. Remember to remove your embroidery from the ring at the end of each work session, so as not to mark the fabric.

Mount larger pieces of work and needlepoint canvas on to a rectangular slate or rotating frame, or, alternatively, use artist's stretchers or even an old picture frame, attaching the fabric with drawing pins or staples.

TRACING THE DESIGN

Using a pencil, trace your chosen motifs from the book on to tracing paper. Then place the tracing paper on to a white background and sharpen up any lines which are not quite clear. Go over the entire design in black ink to give you good strong guide-lines.

At this stage, enlarge or reduce your motifs if you need to. You could do this by drawing a grid over your design and then copying it on to a larger or smaller grid. Alternatively, simply use a photocopier to enlarge or reduce it in size.

Also at this stage, you could digress into experimenting with colourways. Take advantage of technology again and make several photocopies of your design on which you can then try out colour ideas with felt tip pens or watercolours. If you have already decided on a colour scheme for your embroidery, match the thread colours on your photocopy to make sure they really do work together.

You can use your coloured copy to pin on to the background fabric to see the effectiveness of your idea, but remember to transfer the design from a clear black-and-white copy.

TRANSFERRING THE DESIGN TO FABRIC

There are several ways of transferring your design on to the fabric.

1. Place dressmaker's carbon paper face down on the fabric with your tracing on top. Then go over the lines with a sharp pencil. The carbon image will appear on the fabric.

2. Pin the tracing (or tissue) paper to the fabric and baste around all the lines with small stitches. Then score around the lines with a needle and pull the paper away to leave the tacked outline.

3. With a light fabric, tape your tracing to a clean white surface with the fabric over the top. Draw the lines, which will show through from the tracing, on to the fabric with a sharp hard crayon in an appropriate colour. If the tracing does not show through very clearly, it may help to tape it to a well-lit window instead.

You can use this method for transferring designs on to canvas, too, using an indelible marking pen. In this way, you can work the trace patterns in the book as needlepoint designs as well as in free-style embroidery. You simply fill in the traced outlines with your chosen needlepoint stitches instead of having to follow a chart.

4. 'Prick and pounce' is a traditional method suitable for more intricate designs. With this method, you prick little holes all around the design outlines with a crewel needle. Then tape the tracing over the fabric on a board and, with a small felt pad, rub talc (for dark fabrics) or talc mixed with powdered charcoal (for light fabrics) through the holes. Join the dots with a fine line of watercolour paint.

USING A CHART

Needlepoint and cross stitch designs are usually worked by following a chart. Each square on the chart equals a needlepoint stitch or a cross stitch, which is worked on canvas or evenweave fabric.

Remember that the size of the mesh plays an important part in the size of the finished embroidery. A pattern worked on a 10-gauge canvas, for example, will be much bigger than the same pattern worked on 18-gauge canvas.

This design of a path leading through an archway in a wall is worked in cross stitch in pastel colours.

FINISHING OFF

If your embroidery needs pressing, place it face down on a thick towel or blanket covered with a clean white cloth. Cover the back of the embroidery with another cloth, then gently steam press from the back so that the stitches are not flattened.

Needlepoint may need to be stretched back into shape after it is finished. Dampen the needlepoint and place it face down on to several layers of blotting paper on a clean wooden board. Working from the centre outwards, stretch one edge at a time, pinning with rustproof drawing pins into the board. When the needlepoint is 'square', leave it to dry completely (which may take several days), then remove it from the board.

MOUNTING EMBROIDERY

If you would like to mount your work as a panel, a simple way is to stretch it over stiff card or hardboard. Make sure you leave a good border of fabric around your embroidery for turnings. Place the embroidery face down with the card, cut to the correct size, on top. Turn over the excess fabric and begin lacing from side to side with strong thread, starting at the centre of each side and working outwards each time. Repeat this process from top to bottom.

TECHNIQUES AND STITCHES

APPLIQUÉ Many of the designs in this book can be worked completely or partially in appliqué. Combining appliqué with embroidery will bring you some exciting effects, adding texture and areas of solid colour.

With fabrics that tend to fray, make a small turning all around the edge of the shape and stitch to the base fabric with slipstitch. Curves will need to be clipped first. Other, firmer fabrics can be attached with buttonhole or blanket stitch or, for speed, machine zigzag stitch.

QUILTING Motifs with a fairly simple outline can look very effective worked in quilting, and you can then use them to decorate padded items such as winter jackets or cot quilts. Padded quilting is worked through three layers of fabric – the top fabric, the wadding itself and the backing fabric. Synthetic wadding is available in a variety of thicknesses.

Once the motif is marked on to the top fabric, the layers need to be tacked firmly together, either in a grid formation or in lines radiating out from the centre. Then the design can be worked in small neat running stitches or alternatively in back stitch for a more pronounced outline.

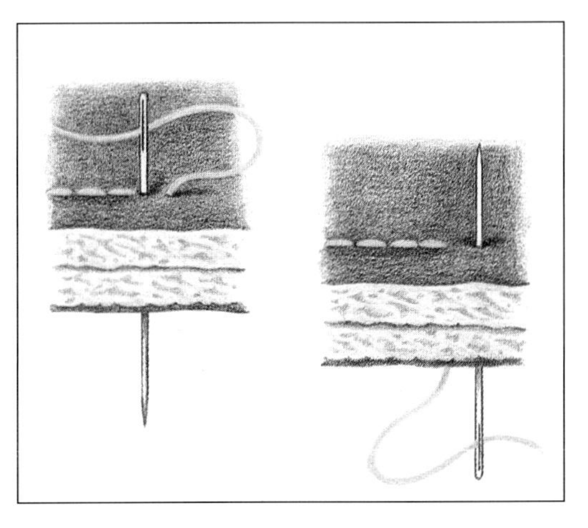

The padded effect in quilting is provided by a layer of wadding sandwiched between two layers of fabric. Running stitch or back stitch as shown here are used to outline the design.

USING WASTE CANVAS You may decide to work a cross stitch motif on to fabric which is too fine for the threads to be counted, for example, a flower sprig on a fine cotton blouse or a denim jacket. You can do this by working the stitches over 'waste' canvas which is made specially for this purpose. Tack it to the fabric, stitch the design and, when the motif is complete, dampen the embroidery so that the canvas threads can be withdrawn one by one, leaving the design on the fabric.

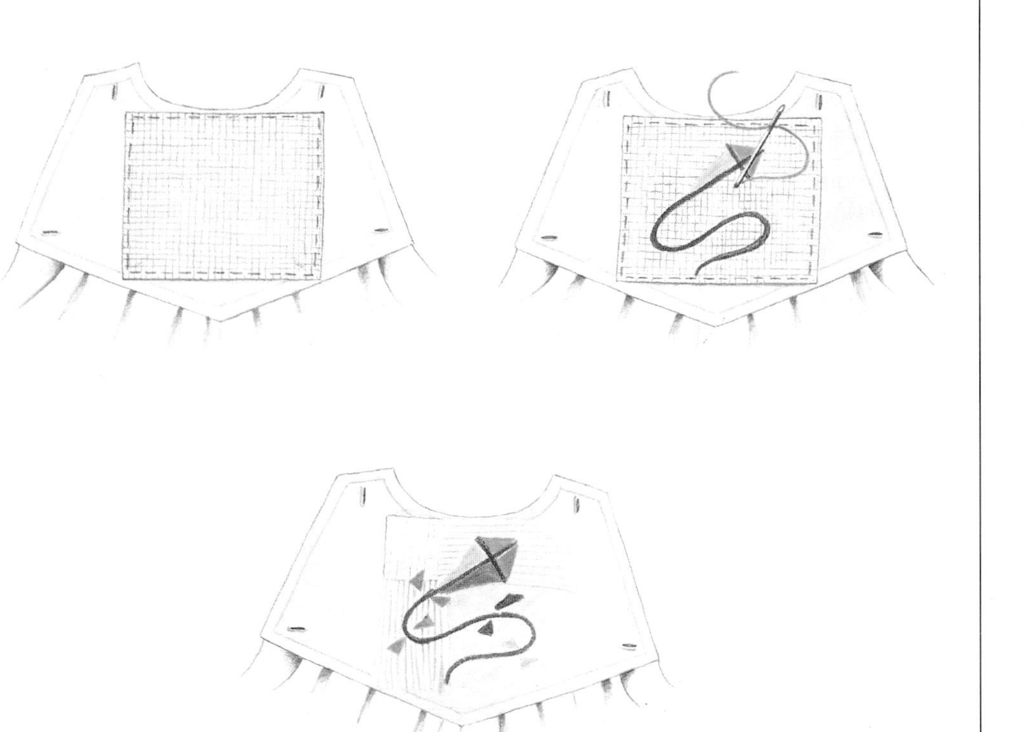

When using waste canvas, tack it to the fabric, work the cross stitch design over it and then withdraw the dampened canvas threads.

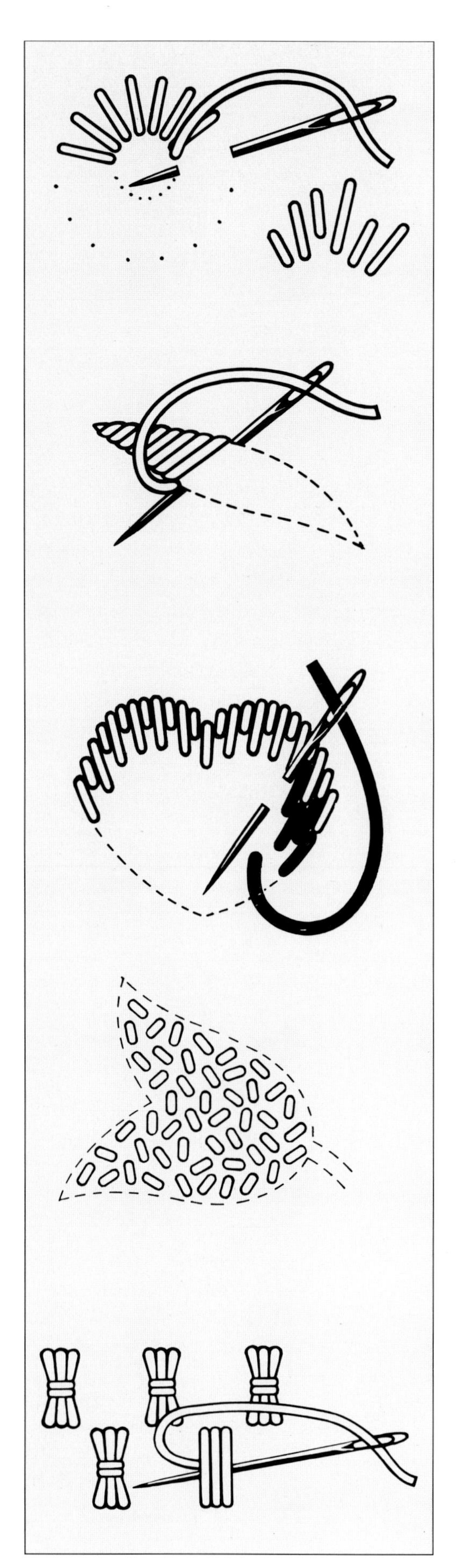

STITCH LIBRARY

FREE-STYLE STITCHES

STRAIGHT STITCH These are single stitches which can be worked in a regular fashion or just scattered at random. They can vary in length but should not be made too loose or long in case they snag.

SATIN STITCH This consists of straight stitches worked closely side by side across a shape. They can be upright or slanting, and may be padded slightly by working running stitch underneath. Satin stitch makes a beautiful smooth surface, and if shiny threads are used, reflects the light in an effective way.

LONG-AND-SHORT STITCH Beautiful shaded effects can be achieved with this stitch. It is very useful for filling shapes which are too big to be covered by satin stitch. Work the first row with alternate long and short stitches, following the outline of the shape. Fill in the following rows with stitches of similar lengths, keeping the embroidery smooth.

SEEDING This is a simple but useful filling stitch which gives a speckled effect. It is made up of short straight stitches scattered randomly over the fabric within a shape. For a varying density of tone, the stitches can be closely grouped in one area and spaced further apart in another.

SHEAF STITCH This filling stitch can be worked in staggered rows as shown or in horizontal rows with all the bundles of stitches in line with each other. Make three vertical satin stitches and tie them in the middle with two overcasting stitches. Then insert the needle into the fabric to move on to the next stitch group.

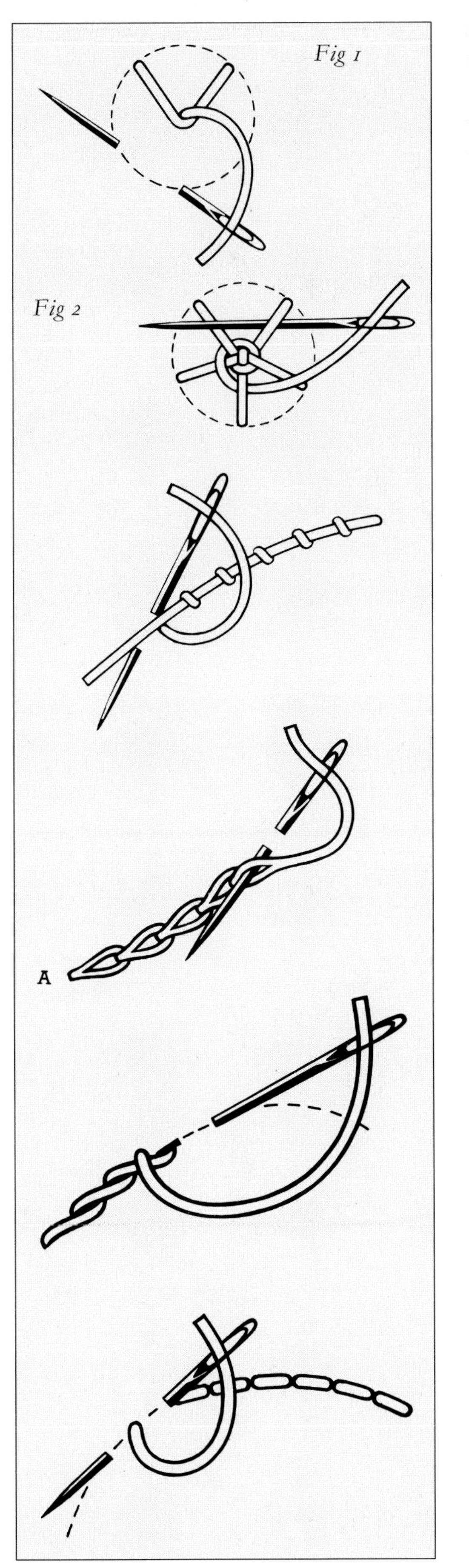

SPIDER'S WEB FILLING First make spokes around the circle as follows. Start with a fly stitch with a long tail, then work two straight stitches into the centre on either side of the tail (*fig. 1*). Weave the thread under and over the spokes to fill the circle (*fig. 2*).

COUCHING Lay a thread along the line of the motif. Then tie it down at regular intervals with another thread, using a contrasting colour or weight if required for effect.

SPLIT STITCH This is an outline stitch, but also works as a filling stitch where rows side by side make a fine flat surface. Bring the needle out at A, then take a small back stitch, piercing the thread with the needle tip as you pull it through.

STEM STITCH This is an ideal stitch for flower stems and outlines, but can also be arranged in rows side by side to fill in shapes. Working from left to right, make small even stitches along the outline, overlapping each stitch with the previous one as shown.

BACK STITCH A basic outline stitch, this can also be used in quilting instead of running stitch where a more defined line is required. Bring the needle through on the stitching line, take a small backward stitch and bring the needle out again a little further along. Take another backward stitch into the same hole as the previous stitch and so on.

CABLE STITCH Work cable stitch from left to right. Bring the needle through on the design line. Keeping thread below needle, insert the needle from right to left as in *fig. 1*. Work the next stitch in the same way, but this time keep the thread above the needle (*fig. 2*).

FRENCH KNOTS Bring the thread through and, holding it down with your left thumb, twist the needle around it twice as shown in *fig. 1*. Keeping the thread taut, insert the needle back into the fabric where it first came out, as shown by the arrow. Pull the thread through and bring to the front again for the next French knot (*fig. 2*).

BULLION KNOTS Make a back stitch the length you wish the bullion knot to be, bringing just the needle point back through at the beginning of the stitch. Twist the thread around the needle so that it equals the length of the back stitch. Keeping the thread taut, pull the needle through and take it back to the beginning of the stitch (see arrow).

CORAL STITCH The knots in coral stitch can be spaced closely or further apart. Start at the right of the design. Lay the thread along the line, holding it down with your thumb. Make a tiny stitch under the line and, with thread under needle, draw through and pull up gently to form a knot.

BLANKET STITCH Blanket stitch (or buttonhole stitch if closed up) is useful for working around appliqué shapes. Bring the thread through on the lower line, make a stitch from the upper to the lower line and, with the thread under the needle, pull the stitch through.

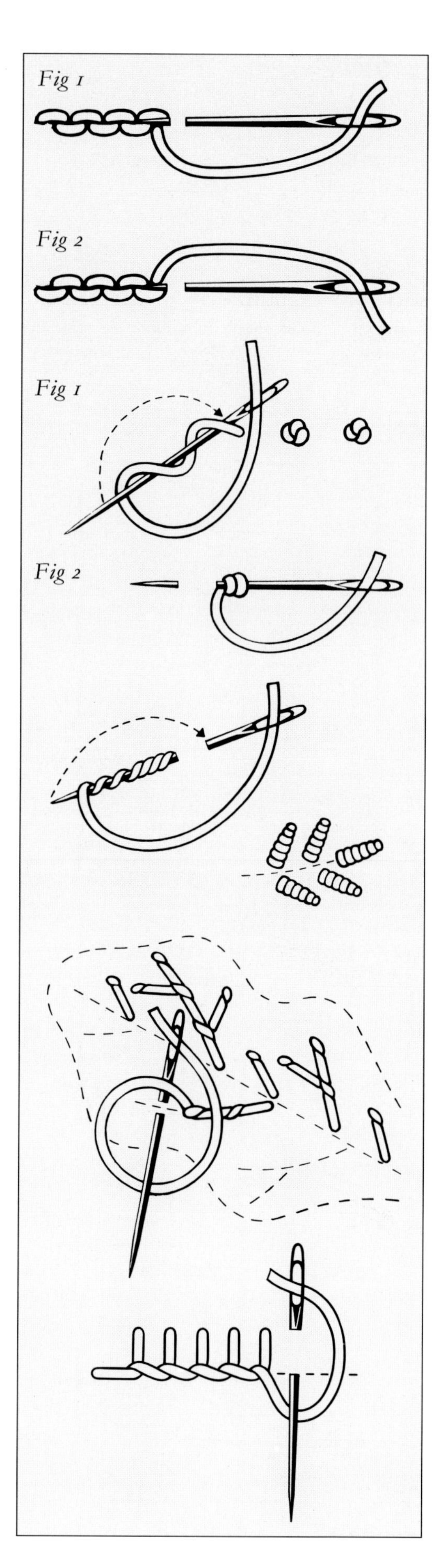

FEATHER STITCH Bring the thread through at the top centre. Insert the needle to the right and make a stitch downwards towards the centre, keeping the thread under the needle. Next, insert the needle to the left and make another stitch downwards and towards the centre with the thread under the needle.

FLY STITCH Fly stitch may be worked in horizontal rows (*fig. 1*) or vertical rows (*fig. 2*), or alternatively as single stitches. Bring the needle through at top left and insert it again to the right, holding the thread down with your thumb. Make a small tying stitch to anchor the loop, as shown.

CRETAN STITCH Start centrally on the left of the shape. Take a small stitch from the lower line towards the centre with thread under needle (*fig. 1*). Then take a stitch from the upper line in the same way, with thread under needle (*fig. 2*).

HERRINGBONE STITCH Bring the thread through at the bottom. Moving slightly to the right, insert the needle from right to left along the top line and pull through, with thread below needle. Again moving to the right, make another stitch from right to left, with thread above needle.

FISHBONE STITCH *Fig. 1* shows the closed version of the stitch. Make a small stitch from A along the centre line of the motif. Bring the thread out at B and make a slanting stitch across the base of the first stitch. Come out at C, then make another slanting stitch across the base of the previous stitch and so on. *Fig. 2* shows the open version of the stitch. Bring the thread out at A and follow in sequence.

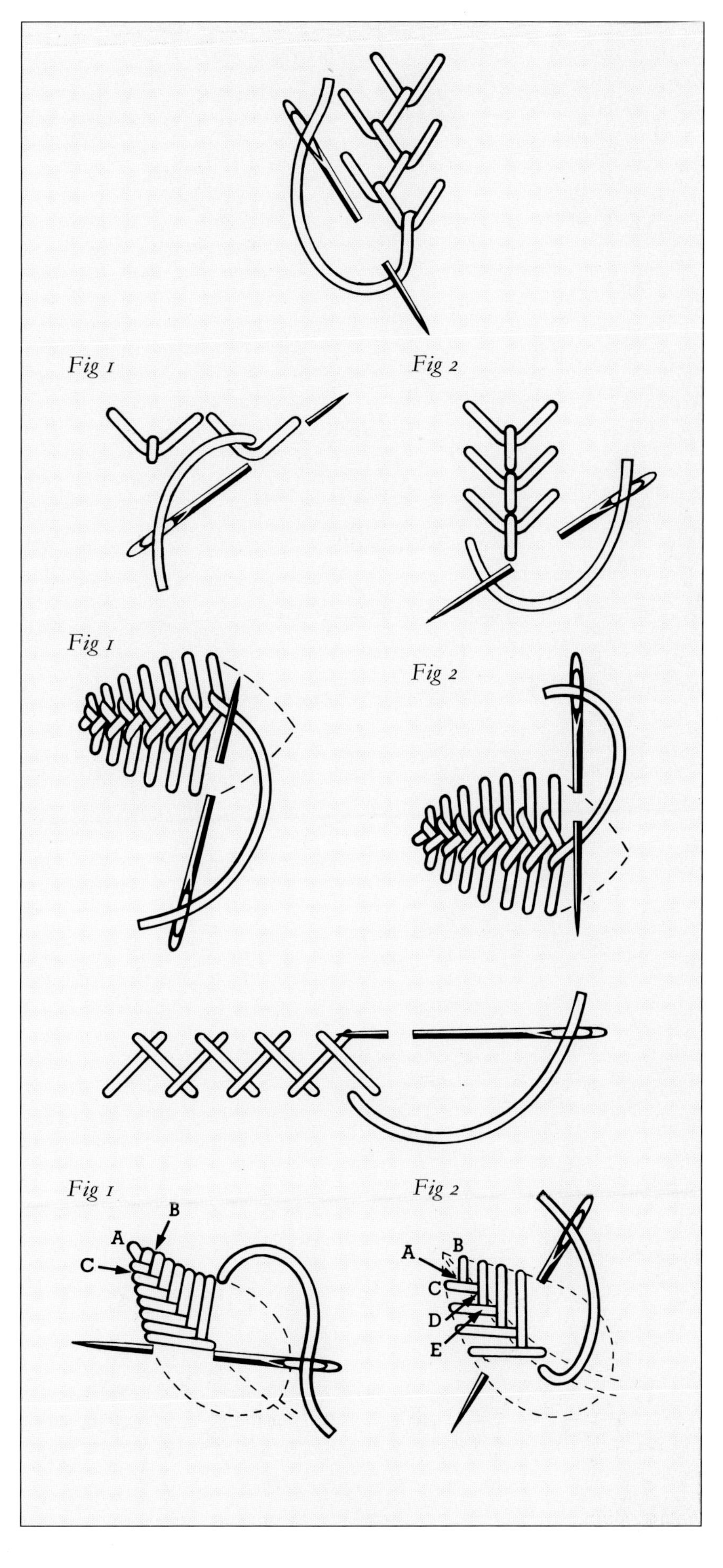

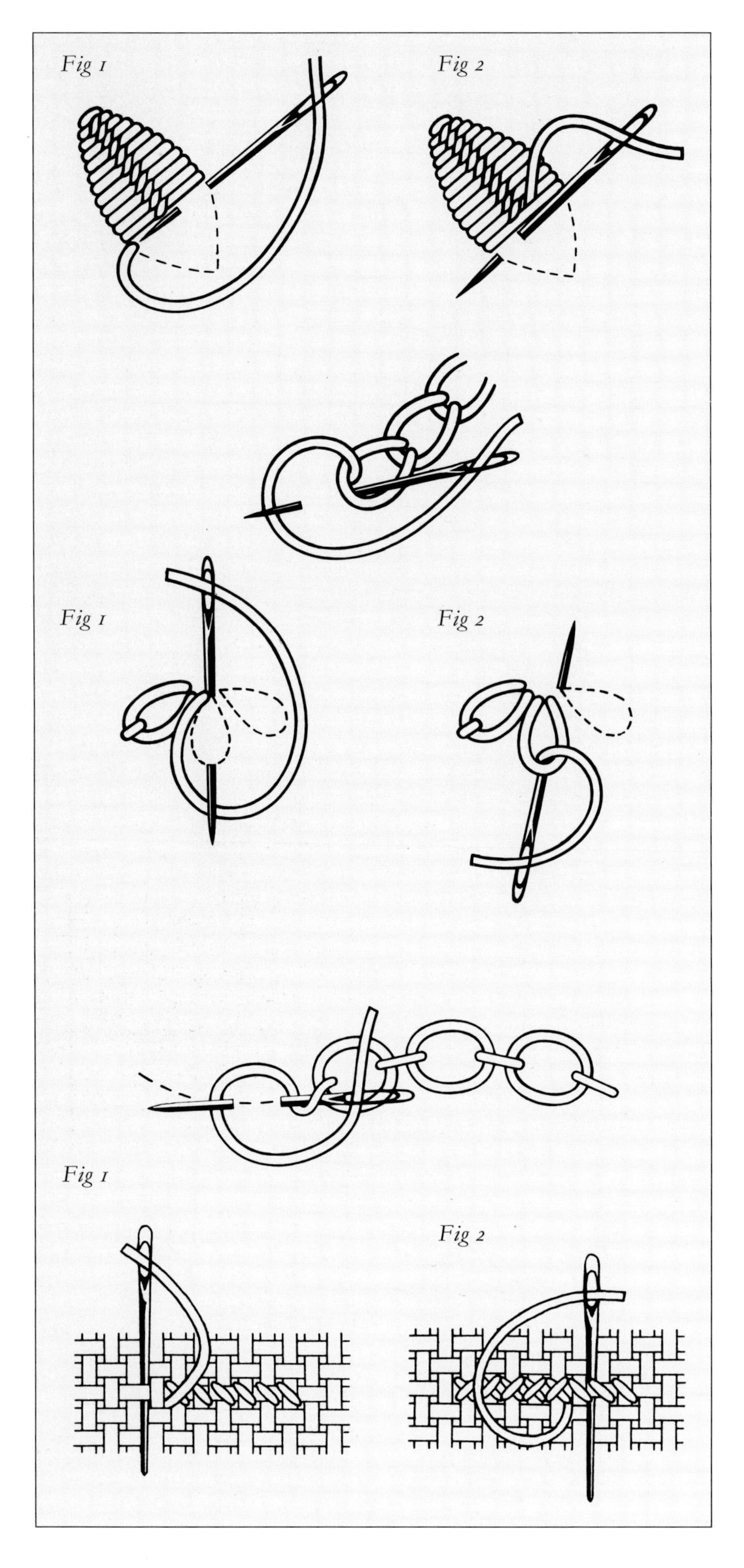

ROUMANIAN STITCH Bring the thread out at the left of the motif, take it to the right and make a stitch to the centre with thread below needle (*fig. 1*). Take another stitch from centre to left with the thread above the needle (*fig. 2*). This makes a small tying stitch as shown.

CHAIN STITCH Chain stitch can be used as a filling stitch if worked in adjacent rows or as a spiral. It is also an outline stitch. Bring the thread through at the top of the line. Reinsert the needle in the same place and, holding down the loop with your thumb, bring the needle out a short way down. Pull the thread through to form a chain.

DETACHED CHAIN STITCH This is worked in the same way as chain stitch (*fig. 1*), but each loop is anchored down with a small stitch (*fig. 2*). The stitches can be worked singly, grouped into flower petals or scattered over the fabric like seeding.

CABLE CHAIN STITCH Bring the needle through at right. Holding the thread down with your left thumb, twist the needle round the thread as shown. Make a loop, hold it down with your thumb and take a stitch with thread under needle. This makes alternate chain stitches and linking stitches.

COUNTED THREAD

CROSS STITCH The crosses are worked in two stages. First work a row of half cross stitch from right to left (*fig. 1*), then work back the other way to complete the crosses (*fig. 2*). The top arm of each cross stitch should slope in the same direction.

NEEDLEPOINT STITCHES

TENT STITCH Tent stitch can be worked either in diagonal rows as in *figs. 1 and 2* or in horizontal rows as in *figs. 3 and 4*. The former method is preferable, where possible, as it prevents the canvas from being distorted by the stitching.

HALF CROSS STITCH This needlepoint stitch resembles tent stitch but is worked differently. It is useful when embroidering with a thick yarn, as it is not as bulky. Each diagonal stitch is worked over one canvas intersection and the stitches on the back are vertical.

BRICK STITCH This consists of vertical stitches worked in staggered rows. In *fig. 1* long and short stitches are worked alternately. In *fig. 2*, the next and all subsequent rows interlock neatly with the one above.

HUNGARIAN STITCH This consists of interlocking rows of a small diamond pattern and is very effective worked in more than one colour. The vertical straight stitches are worked in groups over two, four and two canvas threads respectively, leaving two canvas threads between each group. Each row fits into the previous one.

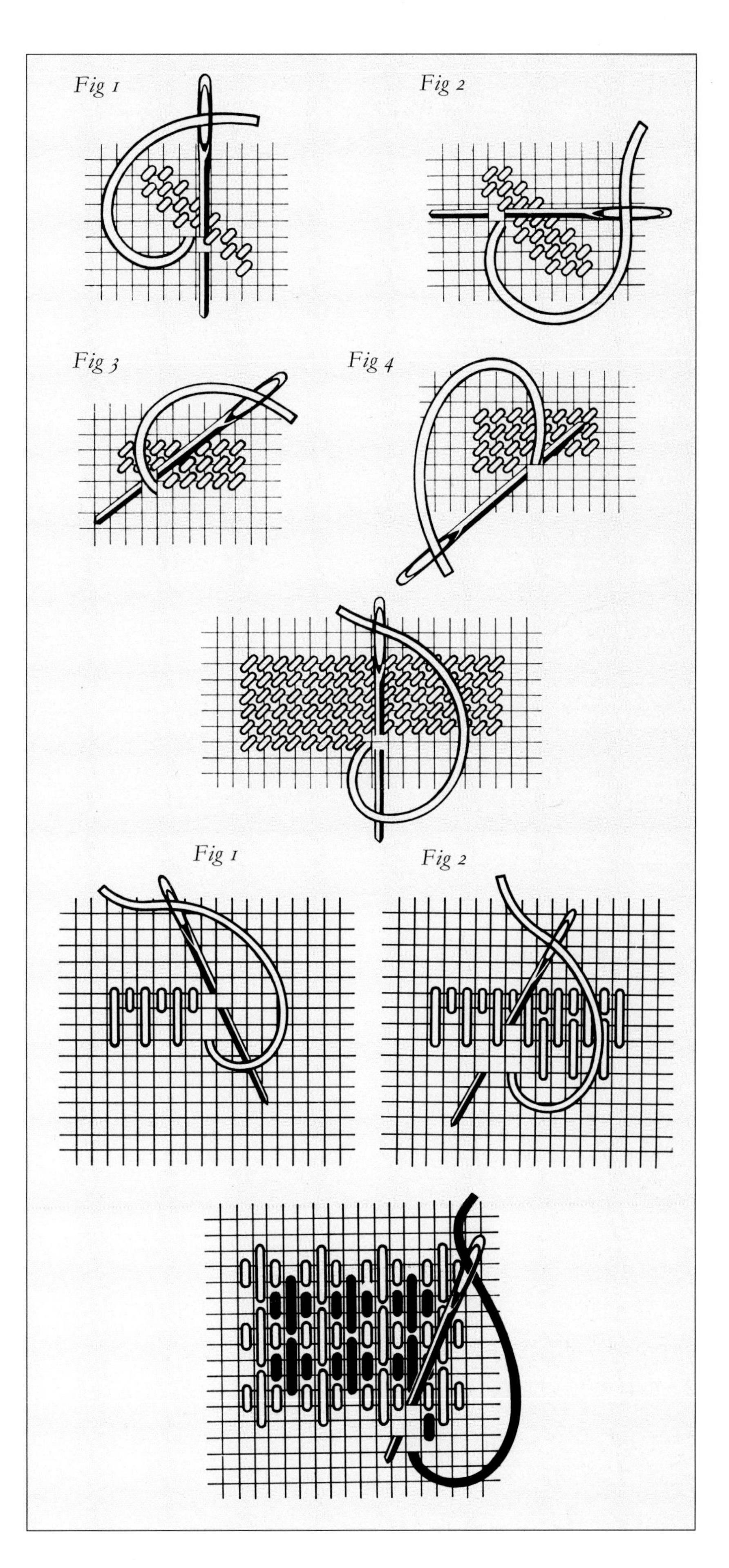

INDEX

The page numbers in *italics* refer to the illustrations.

ACKNOWLEDGMENTS

The publishers would like to acknowledge the following embroidery designers whose work is reproduced in this book.

Henrietta Brooks 66; Anne Carpenter 33 above, 44; Jane Chance Harris 8–9, 110; Coats Design Studio 7, 13, 22 below, 23, 25, 32, 34 below, 40–1, 52 below, 54, 74–5, 99, 111 above right, 118–9, 120, 131, 132, 134; Ruth Collins 64 above; Stella Edwards 55, 101; 'A Pattern of Glasgow' by Gillian Ivackovic, Dundonald Designs, 18 Dundonald Street, Edinburgh EH3 6RY 20–1; Stephanie Gilbert 52 above, 87 below; Sandra Grant 98 below; Anna Griffiths 100; 'Country House' by Barbara Duncan, from *Machine Quilting and Padded Work* by Anne Hulbert published 1991 by B.T.Batsford Ltd 10; Rosemary Jarvis 98 above; Caroline Kelley 2, 3, 5, 11 below, 22 above, 34 above, 53, 65; Jan Knibbs 62–3, 84–5; Gail Lawther 24, 35; Susan Lethbridge Kits, Honeymead, Simonsbath, Nr. Minehead, Somerset TA24 7JX 30–1, 64 below; Natalia Manley, 96–7; Liz Mundle, Limited Edition Embroidery 77, 78, 87 above, 111 above left, 121 above; Lesley Nathan 108–9; Sara Norrish 76, 86 right, 121 below; Patsy North 113; Cheryl Owen 88; Wilma Shields and Katrina Witten/ Rowandean Embroidery Kits 112; Lynn Setterington 86 left; Pamela Smith 43; Susan Smith: 'Country Cottage' in the collection of Carmarthen Museum, Dyfed 11 above, 'The Blacker Morgan Sampler' 33 below and 'Oakgates' 42 Private Collection; Sally Verrall 111 below; Sheila Volpe 45, 67, 79, 89, 122, 123; Sarah Windrum, The Arthouse 50–1.

Special thanks to Anchor for stitching the cover embroidery so beautifully.

The photographs on the following pages are reproduced with the permission of:
Tracey Orme 12; Di Lewis 88; Peter Read 43.
